VOYAGERS

VOYAGERS

The Settlement of the Pacific

NICHOLAS THOMAS

BASIC BOOKS
New York

ST. JOHN THE BAPTIST PARISH LIBRARY
2920 NEW HIGHWAY 51
LAPLACE, LOUISIANA 70068

Copyright © 2021 by Nicholas Thomas

Cover design by Ann Kirchner
Cover images © British Library Board. All rights reserved / Bridgeman Images;
© Arsnova / Shutterstock.com; © Javarman / Shutterstock.com
Cover copyright © 2021 by Hachette Book Group, Inc.

Hachette Book Group supports the right to free expression and the value of copyright.
The purpose of copyright is to encourage writers and artists to
produce the creative works that enrich our culture.

The scanning, uploading, and distribution of this book without permission is a theft of the
author's intellectual property. If you would like permission to use material from the book
(other than for review purposes), please contact permissions@hbgusa.com. Thank you for
your support of the author's rights.

Basic Books
Hachette Book Group
1290 Avenue of the Americas, New York, NY 10104
www.basicbooks.com

Printed in the United States of America

Originally published in 2021 by Head of Zeus in the UK

First US Edition June 2021

Published by Basic Books, an imprint of Perseus Books, LLC, a subsidiary of
Hachette Book Group, Inc. The Basic Books name and logo is a trademark of
the Hachette Book Group.

The Hachette Speakers Bureau provides a wide range of authors for speaking events.
To find out more, go to www.hachettespeakersbureau.com or call
(866) 376-6591.

The publisher is not responsible for websites (or their content) that are not owned
by the publisher.

Additional image credit information is on page 181

Print book interior design by Jeff Williams

Library of Congress Cataloging-in-Publication Data

Names: Thomas, Nicholas, 1960– author.

Title: Voyagers : the settlement of the Pacific / Nicholas Thomas.

Description: First US edition. | New York : Basic Books, 2021. | Includes bibliographical
references and index.

Identifiers: LCCN 2020049066 | ISBN 9781541619838 (hardcover) |
ISBN 9781541620056 (ebook)

Subjects: LCSH: Pacific Islanders—Origin. | Pacific Islanders—First contact with
Europeans. | Human geography—Oceania. | Oceania--Colonization. | Oceania—Discovery
and exploration. | Europe—Colonies—Discovery and exploration.

Classification: LCC GN662 .T648 2021 | DDC 305.899/5—dc23

LC record available at https://lccn.loc.gov/2020049066

ISBNs: 978-1-5416-1983-8 (hardcover); 978-1-5416-2005-6 (ebook)

LSC-C

Printing 1, 2021

FOR NICKY COOMBES-THOMAS

CONTENTS

OCEANIA

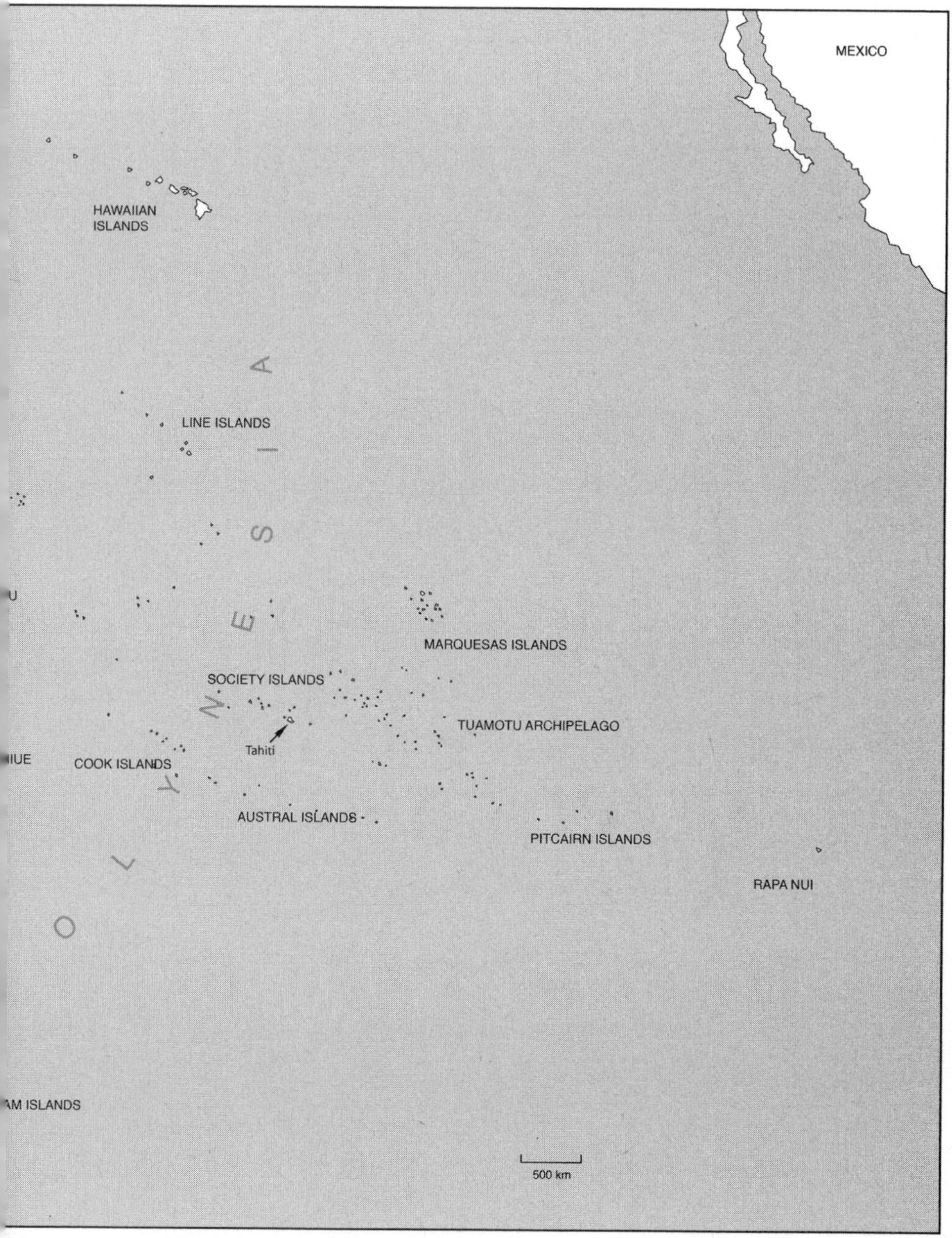

MEXICO
HAWAIIAN ISLANDS
LINE ISLANDS
P O L Y N E S I A
U
MARQUESAS ISLANDS
SOCIETY ISLANDS
TUAMOTU ARCHIPELAGO
Tahiti
IUE
COOK ISLANDS
AUSTRAL ISLANDS
PITCAIRN ISLANDS
RAPA NUI
AM ISLANDS
500 km

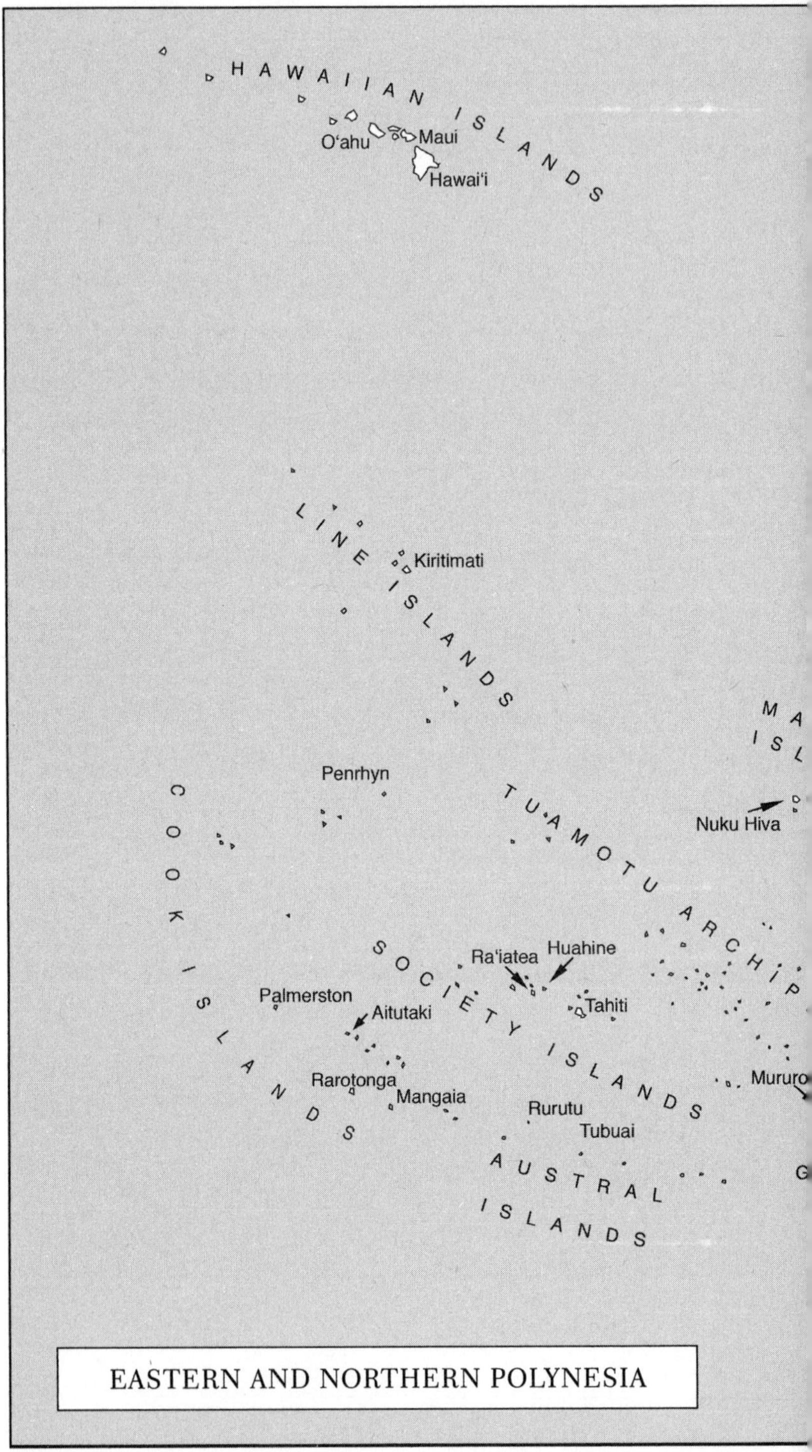

HAWAIIAN ISLANDS

Oʻahu Maui
Hawaiʻi

LINE ISLANDS

Kiritimati

MA
ISL

Penrhyn

Nuku Hiva

COOK

TUAMOTU ARCHIP

SOCIETY

Raʻiatea Huahine

Palmerston   Aitutaki

Tahiti

ISLANDS

Mururo

Rarotonga
Mangaia   Rurutu
Tubuai

AUSTRAL

ISLANDS

G

EASTERN AND NORTHERN POLYNESIA

MEXICO

QUESAS
NDS
← Hiva Oa

AGO
Mangareva   PITCAIRN
ISLANDS
MBIER   ° Pitcairn
LANDS

Rapa Nui

500 km

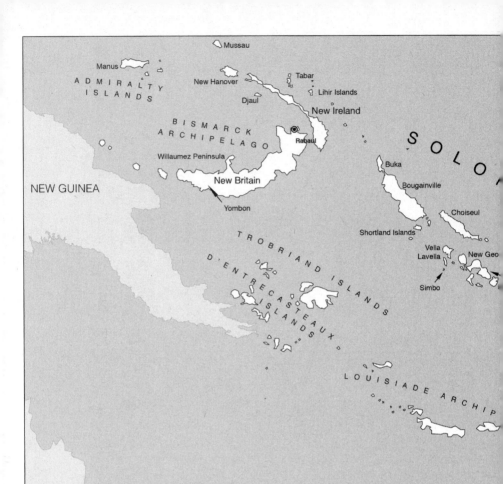

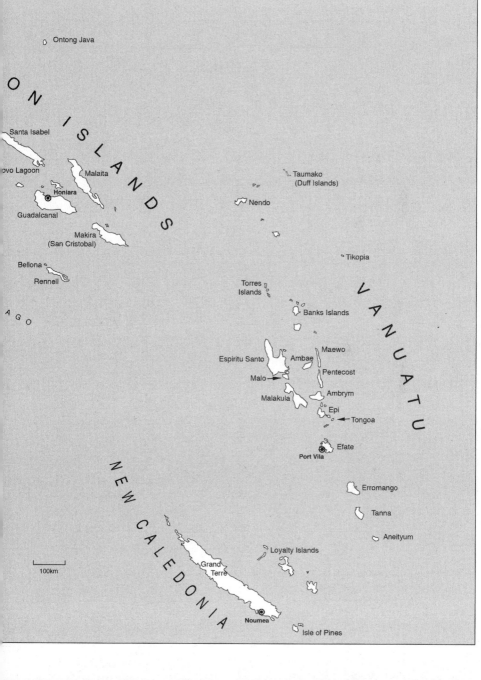

ISLAND MELANESIA

Ontong Java

ON ISLANDS

Santa Isabel

ovo Lagoon   Malaita

Honiara

Guadalcanal

Makira
(San Cristobal)

Bellona

Rennell

AGO

Taumako
(Duff Islands)

Nendo

Tikopia

Torres
Islands

Banks Islands

VANUATU

Maewo

Espiritu Santo   Ambae

Malo   Pentecost

Malakula   Ambrym

Epi

Tongoa

Efate

Port Vila

Erromango

Tanna

Aneityum

NEW CALEDONIA

Loyalty Islands

100km

Grand
Terre

Noumea

Isle of Pines

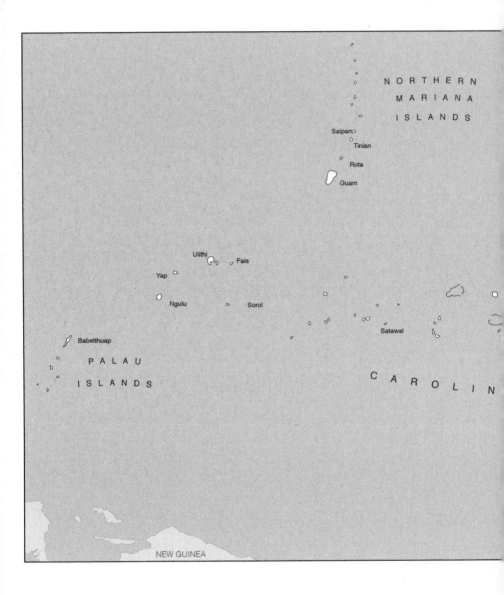

MICRONESIA

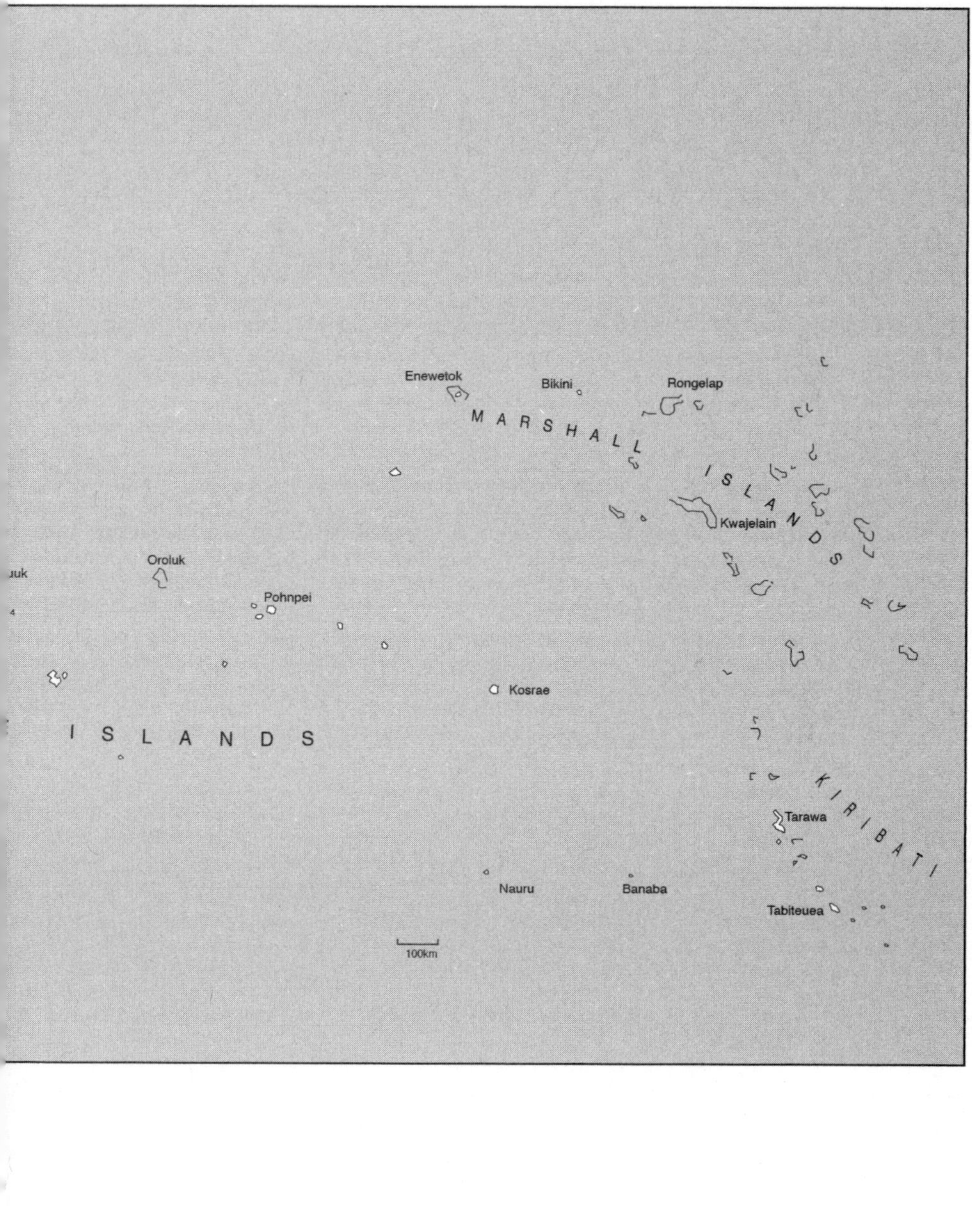

Enewetok   Bikini   Rongelap

M A R S H A L L   I S L A N D S

Kwajelain

Oroluk

uk

Pohnpei

Kosrae

I S L A N D S

K I R I B A T I

Tarawa

Nauru   Banaba

Tabiteuea

100km

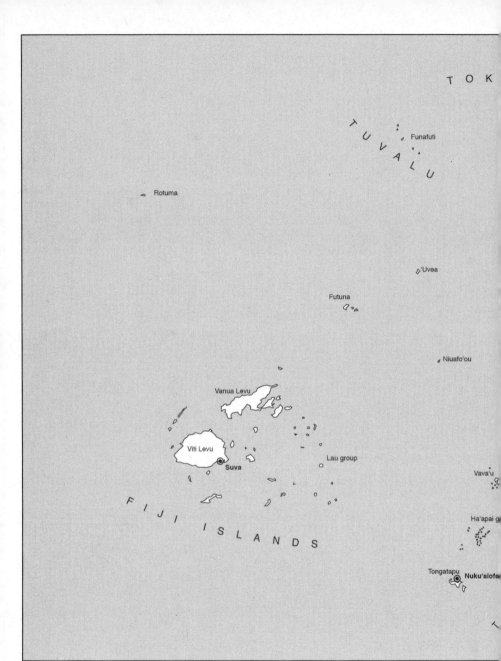

FIJI AND WESTERN POLYNESIA

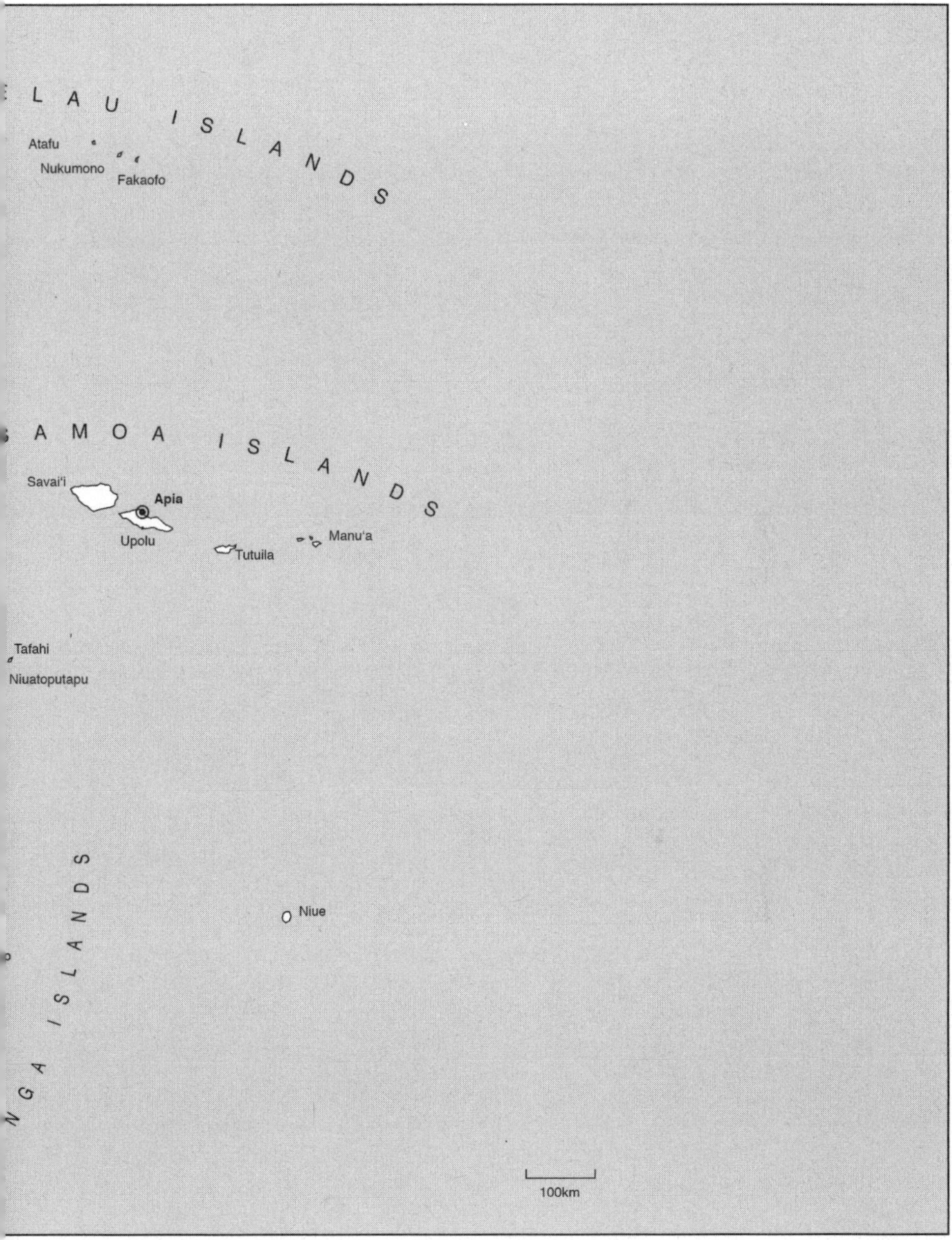

LAU ISLANDS

Atafu
Nukumono
Fakaofo

AMOA ISLANDS

Savai'i
Apia
Upolu
Tutuila
Manu'a

Tafahi
Niuatoputapu

NGA ISLANDS

Niue

100km

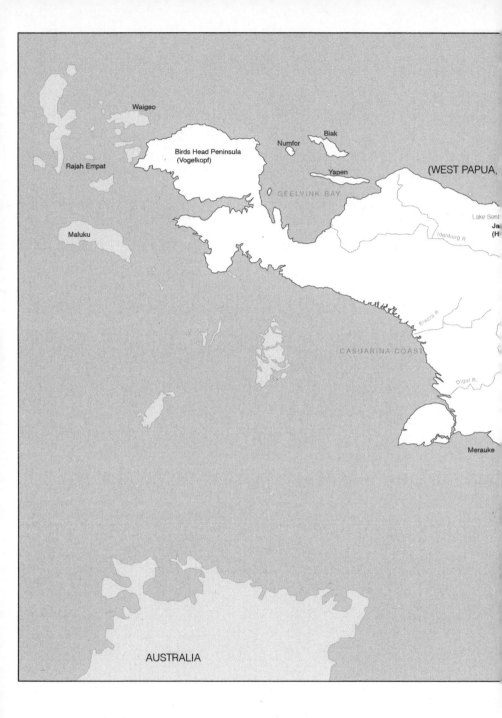

Waigeo

Numfor   Biak

Birds Head Peninsula
(Vogelkopf)

Yapen

(WEST PAPUA,

Rajah Empat

GEELVINK BAY

Lake Sent
Ja
(H

Idenburg R.

Maluku

Braza R.

CASUARINA COAST

Digul R.

Merauke

AUSTRALIA

PAPUA NEW GUINEA

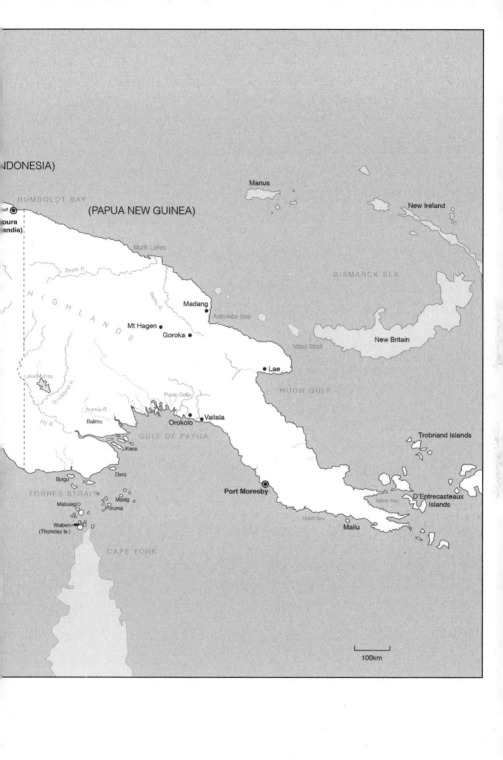

INTRODUCTION

ON A MAY MORNING IN 2016, WE LEFT TUMON BAY AN HOUR before light and drove inland and then along the coast to Hagåtña. Guam is developed, with wide roads, a lot of cars, and some high-rise buildings. It feels like what it, in fact, is: a territory of the United States, with major military bases and too many hotels. Yet it is still irreducibly a Pacific place. As we approached Paseo de Susana, the location of the cultural village established for the Festival of Pacific Arts, it was still dark, but the air was soft, humid, and faintly scented with frangipani. We passed hibiscus on the roadside, and the breeze began to pick up. My ears were attuned to a kind of gentle rattle, a natural percussion of half-dried leaves from the heights of the coconut palms. It was a sound I'd first heard thirty years earlier in Tahiti and had associated with the Pacific ever since.

We parked and walked toward the point. It was just getting light, and the foreshore was crowded with what seemed like thousands of Pacific Islanders—many locals, but others whose tattoos, headdresses, skirts, or shirts with flags

1

or national colors identified as them Solomon Islanders, Fijians, Samoans, Tahitians. . . . We picked our way across coral rock. The sea was gentle, just slightly choppy as the wind rose with the sun. Perhaps a half a mile offshore, several triangular forms caught the dawn. They oscillated, approaching, and within a few minutes outrigger canoes came into view and entered the sheltered harbor as crowds began to shout, chant, and sing. The crews were standing, waving paddles, relieved after days making passage across the open ocean from islands up to 560 miles to the southeast: Lamotrek, Poluwat, and Houk.

Crowds from across the Pacific welcome voyaging canoes arriving at Hagåtña, Guam, May 2016.

The Festival of Pacific Arts had been mounted periodically since the 1970s. In 1992, the gathering had taken place at Rarotonga in the Cook Islands, and its theme had been "Seafaring Heritage." For the first time, the festival launch was marked by the arrival of customary oceangoing canoes that had made interisland voyages. I had witnessed Cook Islands canoes arriving in Samoa in 1996. By 2016, the tradition was well established, but the event was nevertheless momentous. Navigator Larry Raigetal, from Lamotrek, in the central Caroline Islands, Micronesia, said, "These islands weren't just settled by mistake. These are islands that belong to great navigators in the past, including Guam and the whole entire Pacific. We are voyagers."[1]

His commentary resonated with the arguments of one of the most visionary and radical Pacific intellectuals of recent decades, Epeli Hauʻofa, a Tongan anthropologist, academic, and writer, and founder of the Oceania Centre, a cultural institute at the University of the South Pacific. In the early 1990s, Hauʻofa argued for a reimagining of the region he inhabited:

> *Oceania* denotes a sea of islands with their inhabitants. The world of our ancestors was a large sea full of places to explore, to make their homes in, to breed generations of seafarers like themselves. People raised in this environment were at home with the sea. They played in it as soon as they could walk steadily, they worked in it, they fought on it. They developed great skills for navigating their waters, and the spirit to traverse even the few large gaps that separated their island groups.[2]

Articulated nearly thirty years ago, this was a fresh, powerful, and contemporary vision. It was also a post-colonial perspective, an optimistic one that conceived of a Pacific shaped by Islanders themselves. Nevertheless, it was a vision that some of the first Europeans to spend time in the "sea of islands" would have recognized. Among the earliest observers of any Pacific society to live among its people, rather than just interact with them in the course of an expedition, was the *Bounty* mutineer James Morrison, who spent the better part of two years in Tahiti before being captured and taken back to England. Although his imprisonment—first on the voyage home and then in England—was no doubt miserable and the prospect of the death penalty terrifying, it's fortunate for posterity that he was taken into custody. He prepared an insightful early report of Polynesian life, as well as a detailed account of his experience of the voyage and the mutiny, which helped him win a pardon. With respect to Islanders' customary travel by sea, he wrote that:

It may seem strange to European Navigators how these people find their Way to such a distance without the Help or knowledge of letters Figures or Instruments of any kind but their Judgement and their knowledge of the Motion of Heavenly bodies at which they are more expert and can give a better account of the Stars which rise and set in their Horizon then a European Astronomer would be willing to believe which Is nevertheless a Fact and they can with amazing sagacity fore tell by the Appearance of the Heavens with Great precision when

a Change of the Weather will take place and prepare
for it accordingly when they Go to Sea they steer by
the Sun Moon & Stars and shape their Course with
some degree of exactness.[3]

The earliest foreign visitors to the Pacific were astounded and perplexed by the presence of people on islands
thousands of miles from continents. As well they might have
been—over the millennia of human history, our species
has been largely, indeed overwhelmingly, continent based.
James Cook and his naturalists and companions asked:
Who were these people? From where did they come? How
were they able to reach islands dispersed over such vast
tracts of ocean?

A Tahitian double canoe, drawn by George Tobin in 1792.

These questions have been asked ever since, at first by the more curious among mariners, naval men, and missionaries, and subsequently by folklorists, linguists, anthropologists, and archaeologists. From a surprisingly early date, some of these scholars were Islanders themselves. Over recent decades, there has been a decisive sea change in the academic field. Questions of how, when, and why voyages were undertaken have been considered not only in university seminar rooms in North America, Europe, Australia, and New Zealand, but also in community settings and through conversations in which scholars and practitioners of Indigenous heritage—including master navigators such as Larry Raigetal—have become increasingly prominent. New research—driven by a bewildering range of advanced techniques in genetics, linguistics, archaeology, and studies of past climates, among other fields—has generated fresh understandings. The many resulting publications include magisterial archaeological syntheses, such as Matthew Spriggs's *The Island Melanesians* (1997) and Patrick Kirch's new edition of *On the Road of the Winds* (2017). This book does not attempt the deep, but unavoidably technical, review of carbon dates and similar data that such studies provide. Instead, it offers an overview of chapters in human history that are unlike humanity's collective experience in any other part of the world. *Voyagers* is about a civilization that has seldom been recognized as such: Oceania. It addresses questions that have long been debated: Who? From where? How? But it is also concerned with the new meanings that these old questions have. What was it, and what is it, to be an Islander?

The Pacific occupies a third of the earth's surface. It could be described as the planet's single largest geographic feature, and its sheer vastness makes it difficult to comprehend. Seas and waters close to particular nations and regions seem to have a kind of human accessibility that the oceans separating continents do not. On a globe, the Pacific may look like a watery void. This book explores how it became the opposite of that: an inhabited realm. This history of human engagement took people across extraordinary maritime expanses, but oceans are also differentiated environments, with zones defined by climate, currents, and winds.

The ocean's physical structure is the result of the movement of the plates that make up the earth's crust over tens and hundreds of millions of years. The bulk of the ocean is made up of the Pacific plate, which has emerged gradually from the east and moved toward the north and west, where it is drawn down and reincorporated into the magma beneath the crust through the process known as subduction. The edges of plates are volatile, associated with seismic and volcanic activity. Aside from fragments of the ancient continent of Gondwanaland such as Australia and New Caledonia, the islands of the Pacific are volcanic formations—some recent in geological terms and explosively active, others heavily eroded remnants of extinct volcanos.

From the vantage point of the Pacific's southwest—from which islands dispersed across the ocean were ultimately settled by people—a chain of archipelagoes show the boundary of the Pacific and Indian plates (the Australian landmass sits within the latter). That chain runs west to east through modern Indonesia, Papua New Guinea, the

Solomon Islands, and Vanuatu, and then turns south, taking in the Tongan archipelago, the Kermadecs, and New Zealand. It's as though the massive island of New Guinea, now divided between the independent nation of Papua New Guinea and the Indonesian territories of West Papua, fragments at its eastern end, pointing toward the series of large and relatively close islands that today constitute the nation of the Solomons. Many of the Solomon Islands are close enough to be seen from one another, and Malaita and Guadalcanal are over four thousand and five thousand square kilometers in area, respectively. This scattering of islands extends through Vanuatu, toward Fiji, Samoa, and Tonga. Though the distances grow—it's just over a thousand kilometers between Efate, the location of Vanuatu's capital, to Fiji's largest island, Viti Levu—past this group of archipelagoes the dispersal of islands to the east and north is of a different order. Beyond Fiji and western Polynesia, islands are far more widely separated and smaller; though the "Big Island" of Hawai'i has about the same land area as Malaita, it is uncommonly big in eastern Polynesian terms. Nuku Hiva, the largest of the Marquesas, is less than a tenth of the size, at just over three hundred square kilometers. Tahiti, a dynamic theater of encounter between Europeans and Polynesians from the eighteenth century onward, is just over one thousand square kilometers. Guam is intermediate, at some 540 square kilometers.

Most of the islands of the Pacific belong to one of a few types as a result of geological history. "High" islands are, as their name implies, mountainous; they are products of seismic uplift or volcanic action and subsequent erosion. In the tropics, they are often surrounded or partially surrounded by coral reefs. In some cases, such reefs are just offshore, in others, at some distance, creating extensive lagoons often dotted with many smaller islets. Coastal areas may be relatively flat and extensive, with valleys extending inland that sometimes define the territories of particular clans or tribes. Mountains, occasionally active but more commonly dormant and eroded volcanoes, often rise to over one thousand meters. On the Big Island of Hawai'i, the summit of Mauna Kea is 4,207 meters above sea level. The Melanesian islands, the Marquesas, Tahiti, all the larger islands of Fiji and Samoa, Guam, and Yap and Pohnpei in Micronesia are all high islands in this sense, with more or less extensive upland interiors.

The atoll is not only a stereotypical Pacific island of popular culture but also a significant island type. Again, it is volcanic in formation, but it is essentially the vestiges of a high island that has suffered subsidence and erosion down to sea level. The Tuamotu Archipelago to the north and east of Tahiti—prosaically called the "low isles" by eighteenth- and nineteenth-century mariners—and many of the Micronesian islands consist of a fringe of reefs upon which sand and soil have accumulated. Such atolls typically form extended island arcs and rings, sometimes enclosing vast lagoons, open here and there to the ocean beyond. In other cases, they incorporate deep waters as well as shallow basins of coral and sand. On Tarawa, where most of the population of the island nation of Kiribati (pronounced *Kiri-bas*) is located, it is the narrowness of the strip of land that is arresting to visitors. It is generally just hundreds of meters from the ocean side of the atoll to the lagoon side, and the highest land is only about three meters above sea level.

Over time, islands have both subsided and been uplifted, and Niue, in western Polynesia, exemplifies a third category of island: what has been called a raised atoll or an island of the *makatea* type. Made up essentially of an uplifted coral reef, the island is—to an outsider, anyway—daunting, jagged, and difficult of access. Surrounded by heavily eroded coral rock cliffs, intermittently broken up by ravines and caves, these islands have soil that is sufficient to support horticulture, but water may be sparse, as the porosity of the bedrock means there are no surface streams or lakes.

Oceania is an island world, but a far more diverse one than the imagery of films such as *South Pacific* suggests. Though most of the archipelagoes and seas discussed in this book fall within the tropics, the largest islands settled by Polynesians, those of New Zealand, are in a temperate region. Southern New Zealand is dominated by snow-covered mountain ranges, and the far southwest is home to the spectacular drowned glacial valleys of the Milford, Doubtful, and Dusky Sounds, which were sparsely inhabited at the time of early European visits. While the highest islands, such as New Guinea and Hawai'i, have cooler temperatures across their upland and mountain areas, the dominant Pacific island climate types are tropical and subtropical. South of the equator, the middle half the calendar year is dominated by relatively dry trade winds and the period from about October to April by wetter weather. In Melanesia and parts of Polynesia, this is also cyclone season, when communities are often threatened by intense and destructive winds, rainfall, and coastal storm surges.

While volcanic soils are typically fertile, the plant and especially the animal life of Pacific islands is typically far more restricted than that of larger landmasses, the more so as one moves away from the Asian continent and the larger islands of insular Southeast Asia and Melanesia. Over millions of years, seeds carried by wind, sea, or birds enabled plant life to develop on even the most remote islets. But mammals such as wallabies, rats, and bats were found only to the most limited extent beyond New Guinea and the larger islands of the Solomons. Quadrupeds such as dogs and pigs, as well as chickens and rats, that were encountered by Europeans on many islands were invariably introduced by Islander settlers. The increasing distance between islands also meant that sea mammals such as dugongs— which subsist on sea grasses in shallow, coastal waters and are relatively plentiful in the Torres Strait and east of New Guinea—never migrated long-distance across open ocean. Dugongs are found around the Solomon Islands and New Caledonia, but no farther east than Vanuatu. Similarly, the saltwater crocodile—enormously important across lowland New Guinea as a figure in myth, cosmology, and art, and also as a food source—has an estuarine habitat. Although it is capable of sea crossings, the saltwater crocodile is not found beyond the Solomons other than in northern Vanuatu, where it is said to have been introduced in the nineteenth century, and in Palau, the closest of the Micronesian archipelagoes to the Philippines. On the other hand, the bird life of the Pacific is extraordinarily rich. Sea birds, such as the frigate birds extensively represented in Indigenous art, are numerous, and an absence of natural predators before human settlement was conducive to the evolution of land birds and flightless birds, such as the New Zealand moa, later rendered extinct by hunting.

Across Oceania, the richest natural resources have been coastal and maritime. Reefs and lagoons support many species of fish, shellfish, octopuses, and sea urchins. Open ocean species such as tuna and sharks can be sought offshore, and sea turtles are also abundant. But not all islands are the same, and, just as shallow-water mammals never made it to Polynesia, the variety of fish species decreases markedly from the bigger Melanesian islands (relatively nearer to continents) to those in eastern and northern Oceania (surrounded by wide expanses of open ocean).[4] Where waters just offshore are very deep, as around the Marquesas and Rapa Nui (Easter Island), reefs are limited or nonexistent, and the lack of lagoons makes for sparser marine resources. When rains and horticulture fail on these islands, people suffer famine. Conversely, shallow waters and lagoons not only are naturally rich, but enable sophisticated fishing systems, including traps, weirs, and, in the case of the Hawaiian Islands, fish farming on a considerable scale. On atolls—the most marginal and vulnerable of Pacific island environments—salinity limits trees to those tolerant of such soils, and Islanders' implements, such as the adze blades vital for woodworking and canoe building, had to be made from shell rather than the basalt that was widely used by high-island peoples.

For people in Europe and North America, it may be obvious that the islands of the Pacific are "remote." But that depends on your vantage point. Of course, they never were exotic or out-of-the-way for their Indigenous inhabitants, but rather familiar places, central to the lives of communities.

But, in another sense, the Pacific has never been distant from world history. The business of economic globalization that looms large in political debate today got underway with sixteenth-century voyages such as those of Ferdinand Magellan. Magellan identified navigable routes between continents and staging points such as Guam, which was the first place in Oceania to be formally colonized. Subsequently, commercial activities and whaling in the Pacific connected ports in Europe, Asia, and the Americas. Islanders were kidnapped or recruited to work as slaves in Peru and as indentured laborers in Australia. During World War II, the Pacific was a major theater of conflict, marked by battles and campaigns throughout New Guinea, the Solomon Islands (notably Guadalcanal), the Marianas, and Palau, among other archipelagoes. Both Micronesia and French Polynesia were notoriously sites for testing atomic and nuclear weapons, from the 1940s through to the late 1950s at Bikini, and from the 1960s through to 1996 at Mururoa and Fangataufa. Today, atoll nations such as Kiribati and the Marshall Islands are those most vulnerable to sea-level rise. Among the most eloquent voices in debates around climate change are Islander leaders and activists such as Kathy Jetñil-Kijiner, a performance poet:

tell them about the water—how we have seen
    it rising
flooding across our cemeteries
gushing over the sea walls
and crashing against our homes

Tell them what it's like
to see the entire ocean__level__with the land[5]

Oceania has been intimately, perhaps surprisingly, connected with these world-historical events and developments over the last five hundred years through colonialism. While deep cultural affinities among Pacific peoples are prominent on occasions such as the Festival of Pacific Arts, colonial expansion divided and fragmented the inhabitants of the region into formally constituted territories and states. A bewildering range of European, American, and Asian nations have at one time or another claimed sovereignty over, governed, and exploited Pacific peoples. As noted, Guam was the first such colony in the 1660s, serving as a staging point between Spanish possessions in the Philippines and in Central and South America. Around the same time, the Dutch East India Company assumed control of the territory of the Sultanate of Tidore, considered to include much of New Guinea. Many subsequent Spanish, Dutch, French, British, and American navigators and naval officers raised the flag on hundreds of different islands across Oceania. Often their claims were never even officially noted, let alone asserted or acted upon by the powers in question. But, toward the end of the nineteenth century, trade and Christian missionary activity led to the establishment of informal mariners' port settlements, plantations, other colonial enterprises, and, in due course, formal colonial control. The British made New Zealand a protectorate in 1840. In 1842, France annexed five archipelagoes (the Society Islands, the Austral Islands, the Tuamotus, the Gambiers, and the Marquesas), which became French Polynesia. In 1853, France also took possession of New Caledonia, which was used as a penal colony. The "cession" of Fiji to Britain was negotiated in 1874. Then, throughout the 1880s and 1890s, there was a scramble for Pacific territories, comparable to the carving up of Africa.

Until World War I, Germany held New Guinea and the islands known as the Bismarcks, as well as Samoa and parts of Micronesia. After defeat in 1918, control passed to Japan, in the case of the Micronesian islands, and to Australia and New Zealand, in the case of New Guinea and Samoa. Rapa Nui (Easter Island) became a territory of Chile in 1888. The Indigenous kingdom in the Hawaiian Islands was overthrown by the United States in 1893, and the islands were formally annexed in 1898. A joint Anglo-French administration ran the New Hebrides, now Vanuatu, from 1906.

Decolonization has been more partial than many might expect. Hawai'i is a state within the United States. US territories also include American Samoa and Guam. Rapa Nui is still part of Chile, and both French Polynesia and New Caledonia are locally self-governing within France. Samoa, known until 1997 as Western Samoa, became independent in 1962; the Cook Islands (1965), Fiji (1970), Papua New Guinea (1975), the Solomon Islands (1978), and Vanuatu

(1980) followed. Some Micronesian and Polynesian nations are in so-called free association with the United States and New Zealand, respectively, meaning that their actual independence is to varying degrees constrained.

Recent decades have been marked by political instability, separatist movements (notably in Papua New Guinea and the Solomon Islands), and sometimes unstable governance. New international relationships have emerged. Former colonial powers have reduced their investments in development, while China, Malaysia, and other Asian states have pursued mining, logging, and fishing projects, which have brought investment and employment but also environmental threats and conflict regarding the distribution of revenue from such ventures. The twenty-first century's opening decades have been marked by new opportunities but also by major threats—most particularly the environmental threats cited by Jetñil-Kijiner. These challenges may appear typical of the postcolonial world, but anyone who travels in the Pacific can only be impressed and inspired by the extent to which Islanders remain, in a profound sense, themselves. It involves identification with the local environment, with their island homes. But, across Oceania, it also means a capacity to move between islands. Everywhere, Larry Raigetal's words are salient: "We are voyagers."

1

"THE SAME NATION"

Theories and Myths of Pacific Settlement

For over two hundred and fifty years, Europeans knew of the Pacific but knew nothing *about* it. In September 1513, the Spanish conquistador Vasco Núñez de Balboa crossed the Isthmus of Panama and caught sight of the sea from high ground. Struggling through jungle, and killing Indigenous peoples along the way, he and his companions descended to the coast, where he famously waded into the water and, knee-deep, claimed possession of what he called the Mar del Sur, the "South Sea," and all the lands adjoining it in the name of the Spanish Crown.

Even as late as the eighteenth century, the Pacific was widely referred to as the South Sea, singular. Some seamen's charts of Central America and the Isthmus of Panama called the waters of the Gulf of Mexico and the Caribbean the "North Sea"—they were to the north of the part of the isthmus that Balboa had crossed—and those on the Pacific side the "South Sea." The word "ocean" was not used; there to the west of what became Spanish America.

Within a decade of Balboa's crossing, the Portuguese soldier, adventurer, and navigator Ferdinand Magellan had persuaded Charles—the young king of Spain and Holy Roman emperor whose dominions encompassed the Netherlands, Germany, and northern Italy—to authorize and finance a fleet of five vessels that would sail westward from the Atlantic to the East Indies, in present-day Indonesia. Known then as the Spice Islands, the East Indies were a source of botanical gold, much like the wealth in precious metal looted and mined from the Americas. Magellan was in no way prepared for the great distance of the Pacific crossing, and dozens of men died of scurvy, the illness caused by a deficiency of vitamin C that frequently afflicted mariners. In March 1521, the vessels eventually came upon the island of Guam, in the archipelago now known as the Marianas, more than nine thousand miles from the tip of South America. Following a series of brief and violent encounters with the Indigenous people of Guam, the Spanish expedition went on to the Philippines. Seeking to impose Christianity, Magellan was killed while assaulting the people of the island of Mactan some six weeks later. Just one ship, and fewer than twenty men, eventually returned to Spain in September 1522.[1]

Europeans had thus undertaken the first sea voyage around the entire world, but without making landfall in any of the more extensive archipelagoes of Polynesia. Magellan sailed neither as far north as the Hawaiian Islands, nor as far south as the Society Islands or the Cook Islands. Toward the end of the fifteenth century and at the beginning of the six-teenth, other voyagers such as Pedro Fernández de Quirós and Álvaro de Mendaña de Neira (known as Mendaña) made brief stops in the Marquesas and parts of the Solomon Islands.[2] But the Spanish, following Magellan's inauspicious landing at Guam, established only one regular sailing route to link what became the Philippines colonies with Mexico, and Guam became a vital staging point on that long passage. Unfortunately for the Chamorro, Guam's Indigenous people, the island was the first in the Pacific to be colonized, with the arrival of priests and Spanish forces in the 1660s. Soon afterward, local uprisings were harshly suppressed and a smallpox epidemic devastated the population.

The Spanish exhibited little curiosity regarding the Chamorro; they did not inquire into the people's origins or histories. Shortly after the invasion and wave of disease, however, a rather different traveler had the opportunity to witness something of the people and their way of life. The English buccaneer, adventurer, and writer William Dampier was around thirty-four years of age when, in the company of Captain Charles Swan, he brought a fractious crew, short of provisions, to Guam from Mexico on the *Cygnet*. Dampier hungered for new scientific observations of all kinds, of people and of the natural world. His time was that of the founding figures in experimental philosophy, mathematics, astronomy, and natural history who became the luminaries of the Royal Society. In 1686, he was half a world away from these scholars and their deliberations, but nevertheless, in the spirit of this emerging, inquisitive ethos, he took it upon himself to describe fully and precisely the plants, animals, and people he encountered. Following his time on Guam, he wrote at length about the coconut: the use of the flesh, the "liquor" or milk, the oil, and the shell. This was not the earliest account of the tree and its uses, but it was far more extensive than earlier descriptions and was one of the first essays on what might be called Pacific ethnobotany—the profound, intimate, and inventive practical knowledge of trees and plants that the peoples of the Pacific had developed over millennia.

One aspect of this knowledge is especially salient to the theme of this book. Dampier mentioned that "the Husk of the Shell is of great use to make Cables." He goes on:

> For the dry Husk is full of small Strings and Threads; which being beaten, become soft, and the other Substance which was mixt among it falls away like Sawdust, leaving only the Strings. These are afterwards spun into long Yarns, and twisted up into Balls for Convenience: and many of these Rope-Yarns joined together make good Cables.[3]

Rope made from coconut fiber was made and used across the Indian Ocean, on the islands of Southeast Asia, and in the Pacific. Known as coir (probably a corruption of a Malay term), its strength led to its manufacture in Europe and elsewhere. For Pacific Islanders, likely for thousands of years, the fiber was indispensable, not only to the practical business of building houses and canoes, but also to more ceremonial and spiritual matters. It was, for example, woven around god images, binding in their spiritual power, or mana. Lashing and knotting were not merely technical operations, but forms of ritual design and aesthetic work. Fibers were brought together with exemplary tightness, regularity, and smoothness, generating geometric forms that sometimes echoed not only the related arts of weaving (of fine mats and baskets, for example) but those of tattoos. In recognizing the strength and quality of coir in Guam, Dampier had stumbled upon a far larger subject than he realized, involving matters of belief and cosmology as well as technology.

The English visitor had a good deal to say, too, about Chamorro canoes, and about the violence and antipathy that marked relationships between colonizers and Islanders

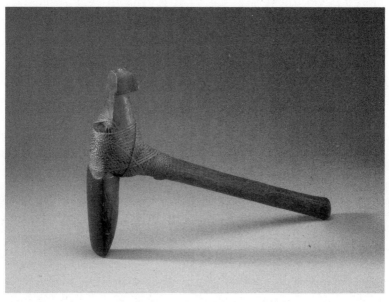

Tahitian adze, with coconut-fiber binding, collected during the voyages of Captain James Cook.

as early as the late seventeenth century. One thing that Dampier could not observe or consider was any affinity between the Chamorro and the peoples of other islands— neither those of the closer north-south archipelago known as the Marianas, nor those of the wider region of Oceania's northwest, incorporating the Marshall Islands, the Caroline Islands, Kiribati, and others. Like the Spanish, Dampier's knowledge of the Pacific consisted solely of the long sea passage from the Americas; he knew nothing of the many islands along the way.

This ignorance was shared by almost all other European sailors. The Dutch explorer and merchant Abel Tasman had briefly visited New Zealand and Tonga in the 1640s. In 1722, not long after Dampier's death, the Dutch explorer Jacob Roggeveen called at Rapa Nui (Easter Island) and some of the many atolls of the Tuamotu Archipelago, to the north and east of Tahiti. But until the late eighteenth century these voyages were few and far between. European awareness of Oceania was extended only slowly and in a piecemeal way. Because they lacked a way to accurately determine longitude, explorers such as Pedro Fernández de Quirós and Francis Drake regularly found islands and then lost them again. In some cases, the identities and locations of the places they had "discovered" remained contentious for centuries. Even as Europeans began to know the contours of the world's greatest ocean, they still knew nothing of the Pacific as an inhabited realm.

For both Islanders and Europeans, the 1760s and 1770s were extraordinary years. The voyages of the British

Society Islands canoes, with elevated fighting stages, feature in this view by Tupaia.

William Hodges, an artist on Cook's second voyage, was the first to paint the famous Rapa Nui statues.

23

explorer Captain James Cook and his predecessors, contemporaries, and successors—among them Samuel Wallis,
Louis-Antoine de Bougainville, Alessandro Malaspina,
William Bligh, and George Vancouver—generated new engagement with and understanding of Oceania. Cook's expeditions were marked by contacts between mariners and
Islanders that in some cases were brief and might seem of
comparatively minor historic importance. In other cases, interactions were sustained—for example, some Maori were
visited five times over the course of the three voyages. To
suggest that these meetings were of deep and pervasive importance, however, may risk contributing to a long-standing
and problematic tradition of celebrating Cook as a hero of
the British Empire. From almost immediately after the mariner's death until today, Cook has been represented and celebrated to an extravagant extent. Though criticism of the
navigator's conduct also dates back to the eighteenth century, it is not at all surprising that Islander scholars and intellectuals, such as the late Epeli Hau'ofa, wearied of Cook
being cited as a founding figure in Pacific history.[4]

Nonetheless, his voyages were extraordinarily significant, although for reasons that have little to do with Cook's
personality and the enduringly contentious questions of
whether his disposition toward Indigenous peoples was essentially humane or invasive and murderous. What was of
decisive importance was that Cook and those who sailed
with him visited an unprecedented range of islands across
the north and south Pacific. And the seamen, artists, and
scientists who accompanied him included individuals with

interests and imaginations that were wide-ranging, indeed remarkable—even by the standards of the Enlightenment.

The first of Cook's three Pacific voyages departed from England in August 1768 in a single ship, the *Endeavour*. Its declared purpose was to observe the transit of Venus from Tahiti, the largest of the Society Islands (after the Royal Society, celebrating the institution's promotion of new knowledge), which had been recently discovered—for Europeans—by Cook's predecessor, Samuel Wallis. Following the end of the Seven Years' War in 1763, Europe was unusually at peace. This had facilitated a period of international scientific collaboration, permitting mathematicians and astronomers to mount a coordinated effort to make precise observations of the transit of Venus from a number of points around the world; the findings would enable measurement of the distance between the earth and the sun. Hence, Cook was leaving England in good time to reach Tahiti, establish a base there, and be well prepared for the astronomical observations to be made at the beginning of June the following year.

Cook also had secret instructions. For generations, geographers had theorized that the world somehow had to be balanced; they thought that the landmasses in the southern hemisphere ought to be equivalent to those in the north. The question might have been merely arcane, but it converged with the fantasies of merchants. Europe's early modern history had been energized by invasion of the Americas and by trade with India and China. The traders speculated about a Great South Land, not so much as a landmass, but as a potential realm of nations and civilizations with commerce and wealth, or, at any rate, a territory bearing precious metals, spices, or other as-yet-unknown rarities. The attitudes of Admiralty lords and ministers were no doubt less febrile than those of the merchants. But the British state certainly embraced the interest in exploration for the potential benefit of British trade. We should be in no doubt that—notwithstanding its commitment to ambitious experimental science and to the enlargement of cartographic and navigational knowledge—Cook's mission was decidedly imperial in design.

Yet the voyage's most important outcomes were almost by-products of the plan. The importance of observing the transit meant that the ship would arrive in Tahiti no less than three months ahead of the astronomical event, demanding more extended engagement with Tahitians than Europeans had otherwise typically had with any group of Islanders. When Wallis had arrived in Tahiti, there had been an initially violent set of meetings between his crew and the Tahitians and then an apparent reconciliation. On this trip, it was necessary that good relations were established between the British and the locals, since the observations could be made only from secure shore bases, which could hardly be set up and maintained without the Tahitians' acquiescence.

Cook and his companions would thus need to get to know the Islanders, and the Islanders would get to know the mariners. This familiarity would go beyond even William Dampier's fine-grain observations. Dampier's books had raised the standards of voyage narratives and represented something of a model for navigators like Cook. But Dampier was gathering information in the interstices of his working life as a pirate and a ship's officer. He was not charged with making observations that were in any way systematic, and what he saw, he saw essentially from the outside. Cook benefited from bringing men who had sailed with Wallis and had some basic Tahitian that the linguistically gifted among his own crew and officers might build on. Because the Royal Society had sponsored the voyage, Cook was accompanied by Joseph Banks, a young, affluent, and ambitious natural historian who was later president of the Royal Society and the most powerful scientific entrepreneur of the epoch. Banks's wealth meant that he was able to bring along fellow scientists, artists, draftsmen, and assistants—the equivalent of a modern scientific team.

Banks's party and others from the *Endeavour* had time to mix with Tahitians. There was notoriously much sexual contact, which may have motivated or aided the British mariners' acquisition of the local language. They were fascinated by Tahitian tattoos, and Banks and others "collected" the work of Tahitian tattooists on their own skin. The extended encounter was remarkable in many ways, most especially for the relationship that developed between Cook, Banks, and the Society Islander Tupaia, an extraordinarily knowledgeable priest and navigator who seized the opportunity to join the ship on its departure.

Over the last twenty years, there has been increasing discussion about Tupaia's role in the voyage among scholars and interested Islanders.[5] It was initially assumed that he was little more than a passenger and occasional go-between, but it is clear now that he helped direct the vessel. He also certainly played a critical role in diplomacy, not only when the *Endeavour* called in passing at Huahine in the Society Islands but also when the ship stopped in New Zealand, where he was able to communicate with the Maori. While it is often assumed that cross-cultural meetings involved a harsh collision of different worldviews, Tupaia clearly understood that Cook, Banks, and their party were trying to locate and identify new lands. He seems to have been positively interested in their mission, and at any rate was willing to share his knowledge.

Tupaia produced a chart that has become an icon of the cross-cultural encounter in the Pacific, naming and locating numerous islands known to Society Islanders, some of which he had previously visited himself. While the map—which will be discussed further in chapter 5 (see p. 149)—has been intensively analyzed and debated over many years, at the very least it made it clear to Cook (who carefully transcribed it) that the Pacific was not an empty ocean but a richly inhabited insular sea, a realm intimately known by able and accomplished navigators. It is one of the tragedies of the voyages that Tupaia was among those who died of fever at Batavia on the passage back to Britain in December 1770. While another Society Islander, Mai (Omai), joined the second voyage, visited England, and returned to the Pacific on the third—thereby communicating something of Polynesia to Europe and vice versa—his personality was different. Had Tupaia lived and experienced something of the second voyage on a return passage home, he would no doubt have shared far more of his formidable knowledge of Polynesian custom, history, and navigation.

Following the time at Tahiti, the *Endeavour* called briefly at Huahine, then turned south, beginning in earnest the search for any southern continent. The ship passed Rurutu, in the Austral Islands, where the mariners interacted briefly with Islanders who came out in a canoe to meet them. The ship then continued south and west, searching for land, and reached the coast of the North Island of New Zealand in early October 1769. The initial meetings with Maori were marked by cross-cultural confusion and violence, and they were some of the most fatal of any of Cook's encounters over his career. Eight to nine Maori were killed within the first few days, and one more just a few weeks later. In the midst of these disturbing, chaotic confrontations, Tupaia did his best to mediate: he "spoke to them in his own language and it was an agreeable surprise to us to find that they perfectly understood him."[6] Others noted that one of the slain Maori was tattooed in a manner that implied affinities with Tahitian custom. While Cook's own journal of the cruise around the two islands dealt mainly with navigational issues and the immediacies of the interactions with people, he and his companions recognized, instantly, that they were encountering a people related to the Islanders of the tropics. How might they make sense of their connection?

Cook's practice in composing his journal was to append a considered set of remarks to his narrative of a day's events, including any visits to a particular place or region. So when the *Endeavour* finally left New Zealand's shores at the end of March 1770, he wrote an extended description of the place and the people. Most significantly, he notes that

they have the same notions of the Creation of the World
Mankind &c as the People of the South Sea Islands
[meaning the Society Islanders of Tahiti and Huahine]
have, indeed many of there Notions and Customs are
the very same, but nothing is so great a proff of they all
having one Source as their Language which differs but
in a very few words the one from the other.[7]

There then follows a comparative table of some forty-five
terms, including "chief," "man," "woman," various parts of
the body, some types of food, and the numbers from one to
ten. Intriguingly, "bad" is listed, but not "good." Although
the transcriptions of the Tahitian and Maori words are not
those of standard modern orthographies, it is striking that
the Europeans were sufficiently competent to record the
bulk of the words accurately, as is obvious to anyone with
even a passing familiarity with either language today. "Come
here," for instance, is accurately rendered as *haromai* or
haere mai, and the words (as ceremonial welcome and as
quotidian expression) are identical in Tahitian and Maori.

Cook was in no doubt that both peoples "have had one
Origin or Source"—an arresting remark given that their
islands were over two thousand miles apart. He added immediately, "But where this is, even time perhaps may never
discover."[8] He was unduly pessimistic, and in any case went
on to say that they had surely come from neither the east
nor the south. He thought any journey from the Americas
unlikely, and already doubted that there was any southern
continent from which they might conceivably have originated, "unless in a high Latitude," that is, very far south.

A year and a half into this voyage, Cook had thus been confronted with a truly astonishing set of connections among people whom he, like other Europeans, took to be uncivilized "Indians." Those people had somehow, in one direction or another, traveled over a great expanse of open ocean. They were evidently related and shared some history, an "origin" or "source." Cook implied that the location of their ancestral homeland was a great enigma, and in signaling the issue he foreshadowed an entire tradition of inquiry into the migrations, histories, and cultural affiliations of Pacific Islanders. Eighteenth-century antiquarianism was yet to give rise to anything like a systematic discipline of archaeology; Cook had no sense that a science of the human past might, in the future, enable ancient population movements to be reconstructed with some degree of precision. But he was also categorical in rejecting any suggestion that Islanders might have come either from the Americas or from as-yet-unknown lands to the south. This was not to explicitly exclude some voyage from the north Pacific, but, given the very great distances involved, it pointed implicitly toward origins in East or Southeast Asia.

Cook's companion Joseph Banks echoed these hypotheses. In the later stages of the voyage, he assembled further "specimens of language," in the form of comparative tables of words from the South Sea (that is, Tahiti), Malay, Java, and Madagascar, which he was able to list with the assistance of a slave born there who was aboard an English ship in the port of Batavia at the same time as the *Endeavour*. While the languages were not as close as Tahitian and Maori, the underlying "similitude" was arresting. "I should have venturd to conjecture much did not Madagascar interfere," Banks wrote.[9] He meant that he could not understand how the "Brown long haird people" of the East Indies might have been connected with "Black wooly headed natives" of Madagascar. He would no doubt have been astonished—had the *Endeavour* called at the latter island during its passage across the Indian Ocean en route to the Atlantic—to discover that the inhabitants were neither black nor "wooly headed." In fact, they broadly resembled the Islanders of the Pacific physically. And, as his information implied, they were speakers of languages related to those of the East Indies and Oceania. The language family would later be known as "Malayo-Polynesian," reflecting that geographic spread; the modern term is Austronesian.

Banks never pursued these linguistic or antiquarian inquiries. Back in England, he soon returned to what had always been his principal interests: botany and the natural sciences more broadly. But during the voyage he had notably grasped a major truth of human history—the extraordinary extent of the islands occupied by speakers of related languages—even as he was confused by an apparent mismatch with physical type. This mix of insight and misrecognition would shape ways of seeing the Pacific for almost two centuries.

The observations made during the expedition of the *Endeavour* would be dramatically enriched over the three years of Cook's second voyage, from 1772 to 1775 aboard the *Resolution*. This time, Cook's mission was to establish once and for all whether the "Great South Land" (presumed to be somewhere richer and more populous than Australia appeared) actually existed. His plan, arrived at during the later stages of the first voyage, was to use the southern summers to undertake a series of cruises in far southern waters, sailing through the seas that had not as yet been explored, and establish definitively whether any land was there. He may well have believed from the start that there was not, and by the time he returned to England in 1775, he was confident that he could confirm that there was no inhabitable land. He had gone farther south than anyone before and sighted the "ice islands" and vast ice sheets of the Antarctic. Between these forays into remote southern latitudes, his vessels returned to the Pacific tropics for rest and refreshment. In both 1773 and 1774, between two grueling Antarctic passages, he called again at New Zealand, Tahiti, and elsewhere. The second of these cruises, from March to November 1774, was especially remarkable.

Like many others, Cook suffered physically from the extreme weather and was seriously ill at the time the ship called at Rapa Nui (Easter Island), known vaguely through the accounts of the Dutch sailor Jacob Roggeveen, who had visited fifty years earlier. (Two Spanish ships had also called at the island in 1770, but Cook did not have access to any written account of that expedition.) Cook's visit to Rapa Nui was significant in a number of ways. This was the first time the famous *moai*, statues of deified ancestors, were described in detail, drawn, and painted. But, in the context of the cultural and linguistic connections that were becoming apparent, what was astounding from the European perspective was the sheer remoteness of Rapa Nui. The Dutch reports had not made clear what was immediately obvious to Cook and his companions: the people they encountered there were closely related to the Society Islanders, Maori, Tongans, and other Polynesians. Yet the Rapanui were separated from those peoples by distances that were vast by any standards. As Cook observed in his voyage journal:

> In Colour, Features, and Language they bear such affinity to the people of the more Western isles that no one will doubt but that they have had the same Origin, it is extraordinary that the same Nation should have spread themselves over all the Isles in this Vast Ocean from New Zealand to this Island which is almost a fourth part of the Circumference of the Globe.[10]

Some six months earlier, in the Tongan archipelago, Cook had been as impressed and astonished by the great double-hulled sailing canoes used for interisland and inter-archipelagic travel and trade as William Dampier had been by the Chamorro equivalents nearly a century earlier.

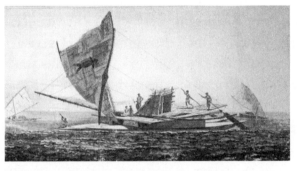

European mariners were profoundly impressed by Tongan seagoing canoes.

The scale of Tongan double canoes is apparent from this print of one in its hangar, from the atlas of Dumont d'Urville's second voyage of 1837–1840.

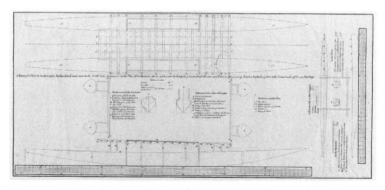

Diagram of a Tongatapu canoe, published with Cook's, *Voyage toward the South Pole* (1777).

Most tellingly, he noted not only that they were "Vessels of burdthen"—that is, that their decking was sufficient to carry numerous people or cargo—but that they were "Fit for distant Navigation."[11] He already knew that Tupaia had traveled extensively and had visited, or knew of, many islands that were variously nearer or farther from Tahiti. What precisely Cook meant by "distant" is hard to judge, but there is no doubt he recognized that both the navigational knowledge of Polynesians and the sailing capacities of some of the larger canoes exemplified maritime understanding and technological achievements of a high order. The visit to Rapa Nui at once confirmed this sense and complicated it. He and his companions were confronted by the fact that people of this "same Nation" had sailed purposefully back and forth across the vast expanses of the Pacific. Such voyages were at the time challenging for Europeans, whose ships were made with the assistance of iron tools and with sails made of manufactured cloth, and whose journeys were directed on the basis of printed maps, narratives, and sailing directions, as well as advanced, if still experimental, instruments. Small wonder that the Europeans were utterly astonished to encounter people who lacked iron tools, instruments, writing, and maps but who had nevertheless voyaged so far. Yet at Rapa Nui, the canoes that Cook and his men witnessed were fit only for inshore fishing. At some stage, post-settlement, the people had ceased to voyage. At this early stage of European interest in Oceanic history, it was already evident that Islander societies did not reflect a "state of nature" but had undergone local change.

Documentation of the Indigenous cultures of the Pacific made during the Cook voyages was rich in part because some of the sailors progressively acquired competence in Tahitian, Maori, and related languages. That is, they were not only seeing but also listening to and communicating with locals. Still more importantly, just as Tupaia participated in the first voyage, Islanders were aboard for sections of the second. They acted as go-betweens, and they were as curious as the Europeans when Islanders were encountered who were different and distant from their own people yet had evident affinities.

As Tupaia had enabled communication with Maori, a young man from Bora Bora known both as Mahine and Hitihiti, who joined the *Resolution* for the 1773–1774 cruise, interacted with Rapanui and Marquesans. Unlike Tupaia, he was not a priest or elder, but as the languages were sufficiently similar he certainly had the capacity to talk to the people. He did so in the company of the naturalists Johann Reinhold Forster and his son, who were keenly interested in Pacific peoples and in larger questions of human movement and variety. They very likely enlisted Mahine's help as an interpreter as they sought answers to questions about both practical concerns and grander matters of history and belief. Hence, when Cook observed that "many of them at this time have no other knowledge of each other than what is recorded in antiquated tradition," he was likely drawing on information obtained through Mahine. He would have learned that Rapanui people had no specific or current knowledge of Tahiti. However, they probably alluded to traditions regarding their voyages of settlement, which may have included names of places Mahine knew from Society Islands tradition, or names that were at least reminiscent of those.

It is striking that, at this early stage of understanding the remarkable movement of peoples across the Pacific, the discoveries made were not those of Europeans alone, but of Islanders themselves and Islanders in dialogue with Europeans. Islanders had always known their own histories, in the sense that customary versions of the past were intimately important in local culture. Traditional narratives of genealogy, voyaging, settlement, marriage, conflict, and ritual were told and retold, becoming part of public consciousness in particular island communities. These stories were no doubt ancient, and they had been recrafted to reflect the ascendancy or decline of particular families, warriors, priests, and other prominent people. Yet in the 1770s, something new began to take place. The connections made earlier through migrations and trade that had lapsed as communities grew were rediscovered through the encounters between traveling Islanders such as Mahine and the inhabitants of the various islands the ship called at—not only at Rapa Nui but at the Marquesas and many other islands. Affinities that had been known only through tradition, maybe for centuries, were revived in practice. Islanders, even those such as Tongans who were voyaging widely in the eighteenth century, became aware of the deep history of connection with the broader Oceanic community. And whereas, as Cook noted, the people of Rapa Nui were at the time of contact no longer making the large sailing canoes that must have originally enabled them to reach their island, from the 1790s on, Islanders frequently joined foreign ships to make their own voyages and to renew connections.

Cook's second voyage also inspired the earliest substantial effort to systematically describe the peoples of the Pacific. Joseph Banks had joined the expedition alongside Cook, but withdrew following angry exchanges regarding the proposed accommodation aboard the new ship, which he considered less than adequate for himself and his team. In his place, the Admiralty recruited, in some haste, Forster, a brilliant polymath and cosmopolitan scientist who is notorious among Cook scholars for his crankiness. Forster brought along his son, who was not quite eighteen when the voyage started. He would publish in English as George Forster but is better known in German literature and history as Georg Forster. He later traveled with Alexander von Humboldt and became a radical supporter of the French Revolution. Though the discipline of anthropology was barely conceived, both Forster senior and junior were inquisitive and ambitious thinkers, eagerly engaged in the observation of peoples and their customs. Following the voyage, Johann Forster prepared a book unlike any other of the epoch, not a voyage narrative but an extended discourse of *Observations Made During a Voyage Round the World*. It ranged over water, ice, plants, animals, and the formation of islands, but it was substantially concerned with what Forster called "the varieties of the human species" the explorers had encountered in the Pacific.[12]

Unlike any previous voyagers, the participants in Cook's second expedition had the chance to make sustained observations of many Pacific peoples: Tahitians, Maori, Marquesans, Tongans, others in eastern Oceania, and peoples of the western part of the ocean, particularly in the islands Cook named the New Hebrides (now Vanuatu), and New Caledonia (which later became a French territory, occupied by people who identify themselves today as Kanak). The terms Polynesia and Melanesia were not yet in use, but Forster placed considerable emphasis on a major distinction among the peoples of the South Seas (by this time recognized as a far vaster Oceanic region than the so-called South Sea—that is, the waters to the south of the Isthmus of Panama, frequented by English buccaneers in the seventeenth century). In his *Observations*, Forster began a discussion of almost four hundred pages dedicated to the Islanders of the Pacific by noting,

> We chiefly observed two great varieties of people in the South Seas; the one more fair, well-limbed, athletic, of a fine size, and a kind benevolent temper; the other blacker, the hair just beginning to become crisp, the body more slender and low, and their temper, if possible more brisk, though somewhat mistrustful. The first race inhabits O-Taheitee and the Society Isles, the Marquesas, the Friendly Islands, Easter-Island, and New-Zealand. The second race peoples New-Caledonia, Tanna and the New Hebrides, especially Mallicollo.[13]

The peoples of New Caledonia and Vanuatu were and are indeed darker-skinned than those to the east, and their hair is curly or frizzy rather than straight. So the naturalist was responding to physical differences, but these differences were coded for eighteenth-century commentators, some of whom thought that "Negroes" belonged to a different species, distinguished not only by darker skin but by "wool" rather than hair. The nuances of Forster's views—and the many currents of observation, argument, and opinion regarding human variety in the Pacific over the succeeding decades—need not concern us here.[14] The vital point is that the observation that there were "two great varieties of people" in the Pacific would prove foundational for subsequent perceptions of the peoples of Oceania.

The most influential of early nineteenth-century commentators on the peoples of the Oceanic region was the French navigator Jules-Sébastien-César Dumont d'Urville, who participated in several voyages to the Pacific and Antarctic in the 1820s and 1830s, two of which he commanded. He embraced what was at the time a novel turn in anthropological thought. He foregrounded racial difference and relied on subsequently discredited beliefs about skull shape and physiognomy to characterize and assess the Islanders he encountered. He prepared an influential paper for a Paris geographical journal, which importantly included a map dividing the "Great Ocean" into regions, including Polynesia, Melanesia, and Micronesia. The relatively mild distinctions made by Forster were amplified into categorical and explicitly value-laden statements that extended across physical type, language, political organization, and other aspects of the peoples concerned. The unification of most Polynesian peoples into chiefdoms or kingdoms was juxtaposed with the

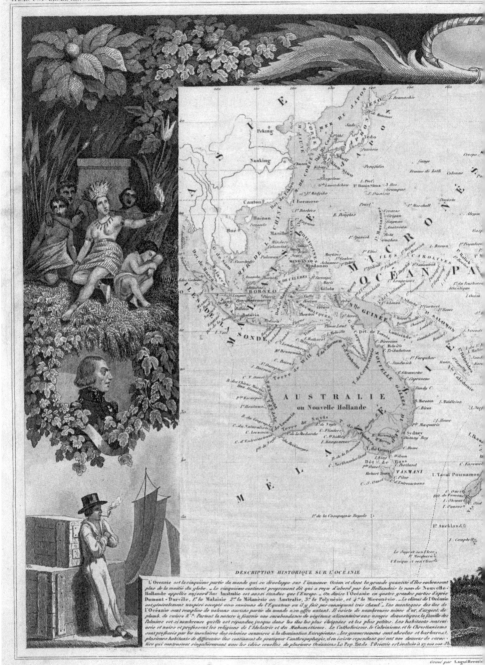

DESCRIPTION HISTORIQUE SUR L'OCÉANIE

L'Océanie est la cinquième partie du monde qui se développe sur l'immense Océan et dans la grande quantité d'îles embrassent plus de la moitié du globe. Le cinquième continent proprement dit qui a reçu d'abord par les Hollandais le nom de Nouvelle-Hollande appellée aujourd'hui Australie est aussi étendue que l'Europe. On divise l'Océanie en quatre grandes parties d'après Dumont-Durville, 1° la Malaisie 2° la Mélanésie ou Australie, 3° la Polynésie, et 4° la Micronésie. Le climat de l'Océanie est généralement tempéré excepté aux environs de l'Equateur où il y fait par conséquent très chaud. Les montagnes des îles de l'Océanie sont remplies de volcans aussi bien que partie du monde a en offre autant. Il existe de nombreuses mines d'or, d'argent de plomb, de cuivre &°. Partout la nature a fourni une surabondance de végétaux alimentaires aux usages domestiques; la famille des Palmiers est si nombreuse qu'elle est répandue jusque dans les îles les plus éloignées et les plus petites. Les habitants contenu-arie et noirs et professent les religions de l'Idolâtrie et du Mahométisme. Le Catholicisme, le Calvinisme, et le Christianisme sont préparés par les inventaire des colonies commerce à la domination Européenne. Les gouvernements sont absolus et barbares et plusieurs habitans de différentes continens de pratiquer l'anthropophagie, il en existe cependant qui ont un notions de caractè-tère qui contrastent singulièrement avec les idées cruelles de plusieurs Océaniens La Pop. Tot de l'Océanie est évaluée à 25 021 000 Ha.

Gravé par Laguillermie

This map from a French world atlas of 1854

divided Oceania up on the basis proposed by Dumont d'Urville.

fragmented and "fragile" nature of social organization among Melanesians. Invidious and overtly racist contrasts were made between Polynesians and Melanesians, ranging over intelligence, temperament, linguistic variety, and the development or supposed absence of law. These included assessments of sexual attractiveness from the male perspective, Melanesian women being allegedly "hideous" and so on.[15]

Maori artist Fiona Pardington used large-scale photographic images to transform the life-casts made during Dumont d'Urville's voyages into commemorations of Islander ancestors: *Portrait of a life cast of Ma Pou Ma Tekao (painted), Gambier Islands,* 2010.

D'Urville's mapping of Oceanic races swiftly received wider circulation through popular encyclopedic works and maps that reproduced the same terms and divisions. The ethnic labels soon became standard. Although the associations and values of the terms varied, Polynesians were typically characterized as semicivilized and Melanesians as more "savage." Micronesia was not so much identified as physically or culturally distinct, but more vaguely as a scatter of supposedly tiny islands—many of which are indeed atolls across the northwestern Pacific, although Guam, Yap, and Pohnpei are relatively larger high islands.

Over the course of the nineteenth century, the Pacific became not only better known to Europeans but a theater of intervention and exploitation for them. European explorers were soon followed by whalers and traders seeking refreshment and local commodities, by missionaries, and by settlers. Colonies were initially of the unofficial kind. Traders established bases and port towns developed, but in due course European powers formally took possession of territories right across the Pacific, particularly during the last decades of the century. The larger Melanesian islands and archipelagoes came under German and British possession following France's annexation of New Caledonia, which became a penal colony in 1853. Both Fiji and Hawai'i were established as politically independent constitutional kingdoms, with governments in which white settlers were influential. But eventually, both were incorporated into the imperial sphere: Cakobau, the Fijian king, was pushed into a deed of cession to the British Crown in 1874, and the Hawaiian kingdom was overthrown and annexed by the United States in the 1890s.

In the context of these colonial relationships, certain Europeans became deeply interested in Islanders' history and culture. Some missionaries' Christian commitments seem to have given way to scholarly interests in ethnology, history, and folklore, and indeed to empathetic regard for Islanders' cultural achievements. Some among them became correspondents of anthropological societies in Britain and provided eminent scholars such as Sir James Frazer, author of *The Golden Bough*, with information about rites and traditions. Some Europeans also wrote and speculated at length on the origins of the Pacific Islanders. The best of these authors—among them the Protestant missionary William Wyatt Gill in the Cook Islands, the Catholic father Pierre Chaulet in the Marquesas, and the colonial governor George Grey in New Zealand—had nuanced understandings of local languages and sought out traditional information from tribal elders over many years. They sent artifacts to learned societies and museums; they assembled and preserved extensive collections of manuscript genealogies, chants, and histories; and they published descriptive books and compilations of folklore that remain valuable for both Indigenous and non-Indigenous scholars today.

That said, many of these thinkers also succumbed to an aspect of the intellectual zeitgeist that remains, in its way, intriguing yet suffers from almost painful obscurantism. Through the second half of the nineteenth century and beyond, both academics and antiquarians outside of universities were fascinated by speculative philology—a history of languages and cultural affiliations—and by the ancient migrations that linked civilizations and peoples over time. Such inquiries were often informed by extraordinarily wide-ranging reading, but they were less impressive from the standpoint of methodological rigor. They tended to foreground fortuitous affinities between names and words. They also arbitrarily decontextualized aspects of rites and ceremonies that were thought to provide evidence of ancestral affiliations between peoples, for example, those of the Pacific and of the ancient civilizations of Asia and the Middle East.

Among the most notable exponents of this mode of thinking in the Pacific was Abraham Fornander. Born in 1812 in Sweden, he was educated in languages and theology in Uppsala and Lund. He suffered disgrace following an affair with a maternal aunt and embarked on travels in America and elsewhere before settling in Hawai'i in the 1840s. He married a prominent Hawaiian woman, wrote for and published newspapers, and in due course assumed senior government and legal roles in the independent kingdom. Early on, he developed what was no doubt a deep and genuine interest in Hawaiian mythology and history, and he spent many years gathering material toward a book, of which the first volume was eventually published in 1878, under the title *An Account of the Polynesian Race, Its Origins and Migrations, and the Ancient History of the Hawaiian People to the Times of Kamehameha I.*[16]

Work of this kind belonged to a broader way of thinking in the West. The premise of much discussion of the time was that peoples were defined by their origins, which could be meaningfully traced over millennia, and that there were vital and irreducible affinities with earlier, formative "nations" or "races." In his preface, Fornander outlined what had become his quest: to trace the history of the Hawaiians "and to pick up the missing links that bind them to the foremost races of the world,—the Arian and Cushite." By "Cushite," he meant peoples referred to in the Bible, associated in ancient times with the Red Sea and Ethiopia. In nineteenth-century usage, Aryan referred to cultural and religious identification in South Asia. It was later recast as a racial concept, and associated with notionally more civilized Europeans, by many thinkers before its notorious incorporation into Nazi ideology.

In so far as he considered cultural affinities across Polynesia, Fornander's observations were reasonable and already familiar to the many travelers and scholars who had made linguistic comparisons. Certainly there was no doubt that names referring to both inhabited and ancestral places were cognate across eastern Oceania: the island name Hawai'i was a variation of "Savai'i" in Samoa, for example. Fornander thought that "Java" was a further variant, which is unlikely, but his claim that the peoples of Hawai'i, and Polynesia in general, had strong connections with those of island Southeast Asia was basically uncontentious at the time and remains so today. When, however, he ventured farther west and north, retracing people's steps back toward the Old World, as it were, his argument became merely fanciful:

> The colour of the Egyptian bulls Apis and Mnevis was black, and in the hieroglyphic representation of the acts of consecrating and anointing, the officiating priest is painted black, and the recipient of the ceremony is painted red; this more especially in Upper Egypt.

Hence the black colour would seem to indicate superior sacredness. It is possible that from these or similar considerations of sacredness arose the Polynesian proverb (in Hawaiian), *"he weo ke kanaka, he pano ke alii,"* red is the common man, dark is the chief.[17]

This style of reasoning and writing is tendentious to an absurd degree. Even the starting point—color symbolism in the culture Fornander knew best—is a problem. In Hawai'i, red was generally associated with great status and sanctity, as is vividly exemplified in the feathered god images known as *akua hula manu*. At every point that follows, Fornander's argument is questionable at best. It is not self-evident, for example, that a priest or person managing a ceremony is of "superior sacredness" to the "recipient." Yet hundreds of pages of what was possible or seemed to be true amounted to an accumulation of evidence that is impressive in its sheer extent. The multitude of citations lends at least the appearance of scholarship. Fornander's thesis affirms the ancient, civilizing force of the Cushite race, who were the precursors of Europeans in the arts of exploration and colonization and "the first to navigate and explore the coasts and islands of the Mediterranean as well as of the Indian seas."[18]

Fornander's work recalls nothing as much as Edward Casaubon's *Key to All Mythologies*, a work famously invented in George Eliot's *Middlemarch* (1871). Casaubon's book is intended as a magisterial exercise in philological synthesis, but is all too evidently a project of theorizing that "floated among flexible conjectures. . . . It was as free from interruption as a plan for threading the stars together."[19] From the perspective of historical and anthropological reconstruction, Fornander's work is—like its predecessor in the novel—ultimately vacuous, but there was work in the real world that the *Account of the Polynesian Race* was trying to do. Without doubt, Fornander sought to affirm and elevate Hawaiian civilization through association with the "race" that he imagined had played such a progressive role in ancient Asia and Europe. Yet he celebrated one Indigenous people by working through the methods and premises of a profoundly hierarchical European discourse. What lay at the very core of his long-winded and implausible comparisons were notions of the distinctness of peoples and races, and a conviction that some of those races were higher, more progressive, or "self-sustained" than others. In the nineteenth century, such ideas were all too often insidious in their effects. They made the colonization and even genocide of other native peoples an inevitable corollary of the spread of "progressive" races. For Hawai'i itself, Fornander's reasoning allowed for the likelihood that these inheritors of the Cushite nation might, like the Cushites, suffer disintegration and be overcome by the arrival, or invasion, of a "progressive" people.

This is not to say that Fornander himself welcomed the colonization of the archipelago that had become his home. His service to the independent Hawaiian kingdom was acknowledged by the royal family of the period, and he died before American settlers and the government of the United States overthrew the monarchy, paving the way for the islands to be incorporated as a US territory and eventually a state. The point is not that Fornander was inadvertently complicit in this colonization, which is contested by a sovereignty movement that continues to this day. It is rather that, however affirmative his scholarly mission with respect to Polynesian culture, he was profoundly influenced by racial thought: the human differences that mattered were racial, identities were racial, a people's achievements followed from their racial heritage, and the business of thinkers and scholars was to recognize and trace race.

This could be said of hundreds of nineteenth-century works of travel, geography, anthropology, and antiquarianism. Fornander's book is singular for the effort the author made to assert—in language that is weirdly reminiscent of debates about identity and the politics of knowledge in the twenty-first century—that he had "a right to speak on behalf of the Polynesian people." He explained at greater length:

> When first I entertained the idea of preparing myself for a work on Polynesian Archaeology, I employed two, sometimes three, intelligent and educated Hawaiians to travel over the entire group and collect and transcribe, from the lips of the old natives, all the legends, chants, prayers, &c., bearing upon the ancient history, culte [*sic*] and customs of the people, that they could possibly get hold of. This continued for nearly three years.[20]

He added that during the many journeys he made within the archipelago, he "never omitted an opportunity in my intercourse with old and intelligent natives" to pursue inquiries. He acknowledged his debt to "Hawaiian authors and antiquarian literati," King Kalākaua first among them, but also David Malo and S. M. Kamakau. These two scholars were both associated with the church and with Bible translation, and they were notable as Indigenous authors of early published studies on tradition and belief. They had in 1841 cofounded a precursor of the Hawaiian Historical Society, to which Fornander later bequeathed his papers. In other words, Fornander drew upon Indigenous knowledge in a very different way than James Cook did. Cook was traveling, and Tupaia, Mahine, and others performed a critical practical service for him as interpreters and facilitators of cross-cultural contact, providing local understanding and insight. Those Fornander employed similarly gathered and interpreted information, but were more like the research assistants who support modern academics, some of whom are similarly more expert and better scholars than their employers. Fornander cited the contributions of these researchers in order to underscore his access to the knowledge retained by local elders and experts. But it also shows that, for his time, he was open and generous in his recognition of Indigenous antiquarian knowledge, which constituted a significant and growing body of locally published scholarship.

The broader questions of Islanders' origins and migrations remained alive throughout the twentieth century. There are too many currents of both speculation and serious inquiry to trace here, but among notable figures was the accomplished and versatile Maori medical administrator, politician, and ethnologist Te Rangihiroa, also known as Peter Buck. Of Maori and Anglo-Irish settler descent, Rangihiroa was born around 1877 in Urenui, a remote settlement beneath the great volcano on Mount Taranaki on the west coast of the North Island. He attended Te Aute College, a mission-founded, primarily Maori school that produced a number of leaders in the period, then undertook medical training and became a civil servant before serving as one of the Maori members of the New Zealand Parliament from 1909 to 1914. Following First World War service at Gallipoli and elsewhere and further work in health administration, he was able to follow his interests in folklore and tradition, accepting a post at Bishop Museum in Honolulu.[21] With the support of Yale University, at the time a sponsor of the museum, he embarked on an ambitious program of what was referred to as "ethnological" research across Polynesia. Through the late 1920s and 1930s, and as director of Bishop Museum from 1932 onward, he was industrious as a field-worker and prolific author of museum bulletins on *Samoan Material Culture* (1930), *Ethnology of Manihiki and Rakahanga* (1932), *Ethnology of Tongareva* (1932), *Mangaian Society* (1934), and many others, building both on his fieldwork and on earlier studies of Maori traditions and artifacts.[22]

Typically running to hundreds of pages, Rangihiroa's reports were empirically exhaustive and rich in detail, particularly concerning the technical aspects of artifacts. He was uninspired by the work of anthropologists based in Britain, such as Bronisław Malinowski and Raymond Firth, who had turned toward sociology and the observation of behavior—notoriously, in Malinowski's case, describing sexuality among the people of the Trobriand Islands, off the eastern coast of New Guinea. Thus, from the perspective of the history of the discipline, Rangihiroa rejected the more advanced "functionalist" thinking of his time, but he was nevertheless interested in ambitious synthesis of another kind. Around the age of sixty, and capitalizing on more than a decade of intensive fieldwork and monographic writing, he wrote an overview of the Polynesian settlement of the Pacific, entitled *Vikings of the Sunrise*.

First published in 1938, the book is engagingly written, a mix of scholarly review and personal reflection.[23] In contrast to his drily objective reports on material culture, Rangihiroa's popular book discloses his own feelings regarding the field and its methods to a greater extent than a twenty-first-century reader might anticipate. He notes that physical anthropology had been held back by the scarcity of skeletal material. "Students had to rely on the comparatively few skulls that had been secretly filched from burial places and had found their way into modern mausoleums provided by museums." At the start of his studies, together with a Maori friend, he had ventured into the medical school at the University of Otago and was appalled to encounter a notice offering money for Maori skulls and skeletons. "We read it with horror and almost abandoned our quest for western medical knowledge," Rangihiroa writes.[24]

For this Indigenous scholar and leader, it perhaps seemed a reasonable compromise to acquire physical data about living people through measurement and examination, which was systematically adopted during Bishop Museum expeditions and resulted in statistics for some 2,500 individuals. In the course of his field studies, Rangihiroa sought and evidently obtained the consent of locals who participated in what critics and historians of physical anthropology today consider a degrading experience. Rangihiroa wrote that "interest in a strange technique wanes, and those who have satisfied their curiosity but have not been measured are apt to go off fishing." On Mangaia, the most southerly of the Cook Islands, he combined his ethnological work with a temporary appointment as magistrate, which meant that he "was able to mobilize the inhabitants by means of native police and to measure them in the courthouse." Under these circumstances, his subjects may not have had the option of going fishing.[25]

These anecdotes set the scene for Rangihiroa's more serious, categorical claim in the realm of biology and anthropology. The "master mariners of the Pacific," he asserted, were "Europoid" or Caucasian, "for they are not characterized by the woolly hair, black skins, and thin lower legs of the Negroids nor by the flat face, short stature, and drooping inner eyefold of the Mongoloids."[26] Notwithstanding his own status and professional accomplishment, Rangihiroa was conscious of the racism of the period in both New Zealand and the United States. He was quite explicit in private correspondence with Apirana Ngata—the eminent Maori lawyer, politician, and advocate of cultural revival—that the reconstruction of Polynesian histories and origins should "cut out any survivals of Melanesian influence."[27] The motivation was to dissociate, as comprehensively as possible, the Islanders of Polynesia from peoples belonging to the "lower races," unambiguously exemplified by the typically dark-skinned and curly-haired peoples of Melanesia. The centrality of these arguments in *Vikings of the Sunrise* was underscored by endpaper maps, which juxtaposed Rangi-hiroa's preferred migration route of the Polynesian peoples into central and eastern Oceania via the atolls of Micronesia, with "the rejected southern Melanesian theory."

The substance of Rangihiroa's book was an exposition of voyaging and culture across the high islands and atolls that he in many cases knew personally. Alongside the narrative it offered—which no doubt engaged the sort of audience who also read *National Geographic* and followed work in popular archaeology and anthropology—the book was unashamedly a celebration of Polynesian heroism. It was predicated on an unsubstantiated and egregious claim of racial identity, which Rangihiroa admitted needed to be investigated further. But he insisted that "sufficient for the day is the fact that a tall, athletic people without woolly hair or a Mongoloid eyefold had the ability and courage to penetrate into the hitherto untraversed seaways of the central and eastern Pacific."[28] The book was initially published by Frederick A. Stokes, a popular New York press soon afterward incorporated into J. B. Lippincott & Co. It was often reprinted through the 1950s and 1960s and was translated into French as well as republished in New Zealand editions. The book's prologue made it clear that the author hoped it would reach beyond readers in the United States to his "kinsmen in the scattered isles of Polynesia": "We have new problems before us, but we have a glorious heritage, for we come of the blood that conquered the Pacific with stone-age vessels that sailed ever toward the sunrise."[29]

In this sense, Te Rangihiroa's scholarship was more than simply a contribution to global, Western-dominated science: it was both by an Islander and for Islanders, for "us," as he put it. The ethnologist was by no means a Pacific counterpart to Africa's intellectuals of decolonization, like Senegal's Léopold Senghor (Rangihiroa belonged to the generation earlier), and he was no socialist, but he was a powerful public advocate of Indigenous tradition, knowledge, and accomplishment.[30] His anthropology was a form of Indigenous knowledge, in a complex sense. It reflected his upbringing and intimate awareness of local experience and customary values, but it also drew upon European disciplines and their methodologies, for both better and for worse. On the positive side, the traditions of careful empirical inquiry, field investigation, and systematic documentation generated descriptive work of enduring importance not only for scholars and students, but for Pacific communities themselves. These are archives of traditional knowledge and heritage. Yet Rangihiroa also adopted uncritically concepts of racial identity and hierarchy. *Vikings of the Sunrise* provides an engaging popular synthesis of Polynesian prehistory, insofar as the subject could be understood prior to radiocarbon dating and the scientific innovations of the postwar decades. But it is a synthesis that illustrates the intimate—and ugly—associations between archaeological argument and the denigration of "lower races."

Another New Zealand anthropologist, Raymond Firth, was a generation younger than Rangihiroa and an exponent of the sociological approach the latter disdained. Firth, who moved to Britain to work under the supervision of Bronisław Malinowski, went on to produce precise, famously insightful accounts of the people of Tikopia, a small volcanic island in the Solomon Islands. In his 1936 book, *We, the Tikopia*, and in succeeding books that ranged over kinship, ritual, religion, economics, and myth, Firth represented both the culture and individual Islanders with great sympathy. People such as the most prominent chief, Ariki Kafika, are intimately presented as deeply knowledgeable intellectuals in the context of their own cultures. From the 1930s onward, anthropologists increasingly concerned themselves with the contemporary lives of Pacific communities and the issues that arose as Islanders negotiated the new worlds associated with colonialism, cash economies, and Christianity. On the other hand, Islanders' deeper histories were, in the writings of Rangihiroa and others, stuck in a murky discourse. This ostensibly scientific realm was Fornander's dubious legacy, where hierarchical premises and ideological commitments motivated origin myths that were at once tendentious and fanciful. But from the 1940s on, new archaeological techniques would begin to bring Oceania's past into view. What would eventually be reconstructed would turn out to be more remarkable than any of the stories that had been so speculatively manufactured.

2

FIRST CROSSINGS

From Sunda to Sahul

WHILE CARE FOR THE ENVIRONMENT HAS BEEN RECOGNIZED AS A vital human responsibility for decades, questions of climate change, pollution, and biodiversity loom larger in the early twenty-first century than they ever have before. In every part of the world, we are conscious that the development of cities and agriculture is having a profound impact on water, land, and the atmosphere; that the rate of extinction among species of all kinds has accelerated; and that for the first time in the history of the planet, human activity is the dominant influence on the environment—hence the term Anthropocene, increasingly used to refer to the epoch we inhabit.

From this vantage point, it is almost impossible to imagine the worlds we now know as island Southeast Asia and Australia as they were fifty thousand years ago. Even the outlines of the map are unfamiliar. The Pleistocene epoch, the last great ice age, began around 2.6 million years ago and lasted until some 11,700 years ago. The periodic advances and retreats of Antarctic ice resulted in sea levels as much as 430 feet below those of the present. Throughout the world, islands such as those of Britain were connected for extended periods with adjacent continental masses. (The English Channel remains relatively shallow, with an average depth of just under 200 feet.) Java and Sumatra, together with Borneo and the now slender Malay Peninsula, were part of a vast extension of the Asian continent reaching south and east, forming a broad and massive hook around

Mer (Murray Island).

Diprotodon optatum, reconstruction.

the great gulf of the South China Sea. New Guinea and Australia were connected by expansive land bridges extending north of the present Australian state of Queensland and the Northern Territory. Although the Torres Strait—now between the northern tip of Queensland and New Guinea—is nearly four times wider than the English Channel, it is also much shallower, in general no more than 50 feet deep.

Yet there were nevertheless deepwater trenches that always separated what are referred to by biogeographers as Sunda (old continental Southeast Asia) and Sahul (greater Australia).[1] Just east of Bali, which formed the far southeastern tip of Asia at its greatest extent, and west of Lombok in the archipelago of the Lesser Sunda Islands, running north to south between Borneo and the Philippines, is Wallace's Line. This line, discovered by British zoologist and traveler Alfred Russel Wallace (1823–1913), acknowledged that the fauna of Southeast Asia was basically different from that of New Guinea and Australia, reflecting an ancient history of separation between the great regions.[2] Wallacea, a sea of some seventeen thousand islands, constitutes a zone between Sunda and Sahul, embracing Sulawesi (the famous Celebes of the Dutch East Indies) and Maluku (long known as the Moluccas). For as long as forty million years, life in Sahul had evolved separately, resulting in the distinctive varieties of marsupial mammals that so astonished Europeans when they first encountered them. Those explorers would have been yet more astounded had they ever seen the giant marsupials that had earlier occupied the continent. Of a whole cast of great kangaroos, wombats, and lion- and rhino-like marsupials, *Diprotodon optatum* was the star. Weighing nearly seven thousand pounds and with a height of about six feet, it was a herbivore and the largest marsupial ever to exist.[3]

No generalizations can be made about Sahul's environments, which included tropical rainforests, tropical seasonal forests, tropical deciduous forests, savanna woodlands and grasslands, montane forests, and subalpine and alpine regions—the highest mountains in New Guinea approach 16,500 feet above sea level—as well as swamp and mangrove forests across lowland, estuarine, and coastal regions. Fifty thousand years ago, all that these environments had in common was that humanity had yet to make anything more than the most limited impact on them.

There is hard data about the movement of people from Sunda into Sahul, but it primarily relates to when, not how and still less why. Even the most basic aspects of when and where are subject to dispute and revision. The who question is also complex. The mainstream view used to be that the peoples who first engaged in sea travel were all *Homo sapiens* (anatomically modern humans), and that this was true worldwide. It has been assumed that movement over water involved social coordination and therefore communication, symbolism, and other aspects of modern human identity, which have not generally been considered attributes of earlier species.[4] The issue is now being reconsidered, alongside evidence for symbolic behavior among pre–*Homo sapiens* species and other discoveries over the last fifteen years. In 2004, a sensational find was made on the eastern Indonesian island of Flores of remains attributed to a new hominid species. *Homo floresiensis* was dubbed the "hobbit" on account of the skeletons' diminutive stature. The remains recovered included those of a female just one meter high, though aged about thirty at the time of her death more than sixty thousand years ago.[5]

More recently, a further species, *Homo luzonensis*, has been proposed on the basis of bones found in deep layers in the sediments in Callao Cave, in northern Luzon in the Philippines. *Homo luzonensis*, dated between fifty thousand and seventy thousand years ago, coexisted in the region with modern *Homo sapiens*.[6] These finds are arresting in the sense that they call for an understanding of human evolution that is diverse and multistranded rather than marked by steady progress toward our own state. But they are also striking in that neither Flores nor Luzon were ever joined to the great Sunda landmass. The so-called hobbits could only have reached the island upon which they lived by crossing water. Although the gaps between the Balinese coast and the intervening islands of Lombok, Sumbawa, and Komodo are narrow and would not have involved passages of more thirty miles, it appears highly unlikely that (at a minimum) a couple able to breed would have swum (or even attempted to swim) such distances. Yet a range of evidence has been adduced in support of the possibility that, following a tsunami, hominids clinging to tree debris might have been accidentally carried across such straits.[7] The gap between mainland Sunda and the ancient, greater Philippines was of a similar order, but a water crossing still had to be made. The most recent modeling concludes that "the chances of randomly making the voyage to Sahul is low except when unrealistically high numbers of adults are washed off an island at unrealistically high frequencies."[8] Hence, while argument around the issue will surely continue, it appears that the crossings were designed, attempted, and successfully undertaken.

Remarkable as their stories are—and further extraordinary details may be added as archaeological research advances—neither *Homo floresienses* nor *Homo luzonensis* had the migratory, expansionist tendencies of *Homo sapiens*. So far as can now be established, neither species ventured significantly beyond the regions in which their remains were first identified. The hominids who would have a greater and more enduring impact were *Homo sapiens*. The species began to move out of Africa some 120,000 years ago, was present in the Middle East at least 90,000 years ago, and was in Southeast Asia 70,000 years ago. As people migrated, they adapted to changing environments, and at times these early *sapiens* encountered and interbred with older, non-*sapiens* populations who had previously left Africa. The earliest migrants into the Australasian region were bearers of a hybrid biological and cultural identity, which diverged from Eurasian populations and acquired its distinctiveness in the Sunda region.[9]

The discovery of carbon dating in the 1940s led to a revolution in archaeological science. Dates for Aboriginal sites in Australia began to be published around 1960, but it was at the end of that decade that scientists made discoveries pointing to a far more ancient history in Australia than had been suspected. In 1969, the remains of a cremated woman were found in the sand dunes on the edge of Lake Mungo in western New South Wales. Five years later, a male skeleton was discovered in the nearby deposits. The woman's remains were dated to between nineteen thousand and twenty-four thousand years earlier. Evidence that her body had been burned, as well as the presence of ocher from a considerable distance away, implied a ceremonial interment. The man's remains were far older, from around forty-two thousand years ago. Immensely exciting at the time, these findings were not only scientifically significant, but they pointed to new imaginings: Australia, conceived for so long as a vast, arid wilderness, was revealed as a continent with a deep inhabited history that had seen ritual for millennia. Yet its ancient civilization was one of nomads, and its deep histories were quite unlike those of other parts of the world.

Some areas, such as the islands of Wallacea, through which humans must have initially traveled, are still to be extensively investigated. But archaeological research across the wider region has advanced dramatically, and numerous early dates for sites situated in what are now the separate landmasses of New Guinea and Australia—as well as the Bismarck Islands, which extend northeast of Papua— have been reliably established.[10] The earliest dates for northern Australia suggest that human settlement may have taken place around or even before sixty thousand years ago, but the accuracy of the dates has been extensively debated. There is a greater density of archaeological sites for the period fifty thousand to forty-five thousand years before the

The Raja Ampat Islands, off the northwest tip of Bird's Head Peninsula.

present; if humans did arrive ten thousand years or so earlier, they most likely did so in very small numbers.[11]

The Huon Peninsula, which points east from the northern coast of New Guinea into the seas toward the Solomon Islands like a massive snout, is distinctive because of its succession of uplifted terraces, raised by tectonic movements over the last 140,000 years. These terraces, now up to 650 feet above the coast, were at one time at sea level. In the 1980s, archaeologists working here found numerous large worked-stone blades—possibly designed to clear vegetation in the context of foraging—that are over forty thousand years old.[12] In other parts of mainland New Guinea, open, swamp, and rock shelter sites date from between thirty thousand and forty-seven thousand years ago. Some sites on New Britain, in the Bismarck Islands, are dated between thirty-eight thousand and forty-two thousand years ago. On New Ireland, forming the northern part of a great insular arc, there are sites that are even older. As New Ireland was presumably reached via New Britain, those older dates should indicate the antiquity of settlement for the archipelago as a whole. In sum, there is clear evidence that *Homo sapiens* had not only crossed into Sahul by forty-five thousand to fifty thousand years ago, but that they had then dispersed across that vast and diverse landmass, New Guinea and Australia combined, and even ventured beyond it around the Bismarck Islands.

The *how* is a realm of enigma in two senses. First, what route might the first voyagers have taken? The most obvious journey from the Sunda landmass to Sahul must have brought *Homo sapiens* into contact with *Homo floresiensis.*

The island chain runs precisely west-east from Bali through Flores to Timor, and the distance separating each island is not great. Fifty thousand years ago, the crossing from Timor to the expanded north Australian coast was far shorter than the passage today. But, in the absence of more fine-grain archaeological evidence (for instance, a pattern of early *sapiens* sites through one group of islands and their absence in the other), alternative routes farther north—through Sulawesi and Ceram toward the Bird's Head (the great peninsula of northwestern New Guinea), or some variation—cannot be ruled out.[13]

Second, what kinds of vessels enabled sea crossings to be made? As there are no boats of this age extant from any part of the world, this is entirely a matter for conjecture. It's worth observing that there is, for the likely period of first crossing, likewise no evidence for any kind of deep-sea fishing. Coastal subsistence was a matter primarily of living off shellfish or other species that could be readily gathered from the shore. In other words, people did not make or use boats for fishing that could be enlarged or adapted for longer passages. The vessels most probably used were rafts or simple canoes made from materials that were not challenging or time-consuming to handle, such as a variety of bamboo. Bamboo has the great advantage of being inherently buoyant, as the hollow voids between the nodes are naturally airtight. A species such as *Dendrocalamus giganteus* (dragon or giant bamboo), which was common throughout the region, grew swiftly and could reach over one hundred feet in height. Individual tubes could be as much as fourteen inches in diameter, meaning that comparatively few, or a

The Wayag area, Raja Ampat Islands.

mix of very thick tubes and thinner ones, could be tied together with vines to form a long but relatively narrow boat, susceptible to basic steering. Even a raft of squarer design could have been paddled and perhaps maneuvered to a limited degree; it is likely that vessels of either sort would have enabled people to cross open water to another land with the assistance of favorable winds and currents.[14]

Given the lack of hard evidence, the use of different kinds of boats, such as bark or even dugout canoes, cannot be ruled out.[15] But it is difficult to see how a people without a tradition of canoe making would have developed boats of this type or been able to stitch sheets of bark together to create a vessel that was not leaky, could weather at least a normal swell in open water on a calm day, and was large enough to carry more than two to three individuals. Assuming a deliberate intention on the part of a group to resettle in a territory across water, a party would presumably have consisted of more than one male-female couple. Demographic modeling of the necessary size for a viable population points toward greater numbers: some hundreds of thousands, presumably arriving over decades or hundreds of years.[16] We might assume that boats needed to carry not only people, but also their utensils and belongings, such as hunting implements, baskets, bags, garments, and items of personal adornment. If the accidental drift of refugees from some volcanic eruption or similar catastrophe cannot be absolutely excluded, the establishment of a population that survived—or, indeed, thrived and spread comparatively swiftly over new lands once they were reached—is suggestive of a venture that was both deliberately conceived and sustained over a period.

Yet those who inhabited Wallacea did not become seafarers at the time of these early crossings. The evidence from the distribution of animals and from genetics does not point toward back-and-forth voyaging, or to an extended series of migrations by successive groups. The relative homogeneity of the population of Sahul rather suggests settlement of this vast and diverse region by *Homo sapiens* through a single episode or several closely linked passages, presumably by related groups.

Relatively soon after—though it is difficult to be specific about what "soon" means in the context—people covered vast distances to occupy the northern and eastern extremities of New Guinea and southeastern Australia. The distance from an assumed landfall south of Timor to an archaeological site such as Keilor, close to Melbourne's main airport, is just under two thousand miles, farther than Paris is from Istanbul. The peoples of mainland Australia became separated from those of New Guinea and, again, biological anthropology suggests that subsequent interaction among the groups did not take place. The history was thus one of relocation—that is, travel that led to the establishment of a mode of life that would be adapted to new environments, some of them utterly different from the coastal or small-island setting. This new mode of living was then localized. It was not apparently part of a sustained or regionally extensive social network, nor were ancestral connections with other places maintained through exchange or any form of inter-marriage. From one perspective, this is exactly what one would expect: while the archaeological record is not rich, it implies comparatively simple modes of localized hunting and gathering. But in fact the populations that moved through the diverse and challenging environments of New Guinea and Australia developed locally specific technologies and new ways of living. The large blades found in the raised sediments on the Huon Peninsula have been interpreted as forest-clearing tools, which would have opened up areas in which edible plants such as sago, bananas, and yam vines might have spread. These people were not horticulturalists in the strict sense, but they appear to have been intervening in the environment to enable edible plants to flourish and spread to a greater extent than they would have if left unattended. If these really were experiments toward cultivation, they took place at a remarkably early date, far earlier than conventional histories of agriculture have acknowledged.

Relative to the peoples who arrived subsequently, these ancestors of Papuans and Indigenous Australians appear to have been less specialized and, inevitably, less dynamic. While it is difficult to paint any finely detailed picture, given the relatively sparse archaeological record for these early periods, there is abundant evidence for distinctive creativity, innovation, and adaptation. Recent discoveries from the Leang Bulu' Sipong cave site in southern Sulawesi have revealed what appears to be the earliest narrative scene in cave art from any part of the world. In particular, a fifteen-foot panel constitutes a scene in which human-animal hybrids—with human bodies but indeterminate, animal heads—are engaged in hunting pigs and a bovid, such as a wild ox of some kind. No specific belief, nor a spiritual practice such as shamanism, can be identified from this scene other than speculatively. However, it has generally been assumed that similar representations from later periods were not just images of hunting, but were part of some magical or ritual effort to enhance the success of hunters, who may have danced or chanted in the presence of the painting. The Leang Bulu' Sipong cave art is at least 43,900 years old. It provides a tantalizing glimpse of the beliefs of the people of the place at that time, and it is presumably an indication of the importance of hunting in their culture.[17]

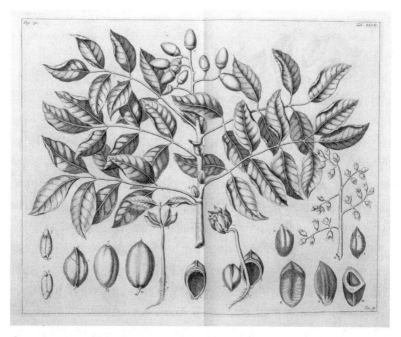

Canarium, an eighteenth century engraving.

Yet at least some *sapiens* groups in the Wallacea-Papua region in this early period were oriented as much to sea as to land. People preferred to live along coastlines, and the earliest foragers no doubt collected and consumed shellfish, crabs, and other species that were readily accessible on reefs and in shallow waters. However, evidence for fishing is sparse from any part of the world before around twelve thousand years ago—no doubt in part because older coastal sites were eroded or submerged as Pleistocene sea levels rose. It does not help that fishing materials such as spears, nets, and lines are generally perishable. Some early Sahul sites that are close to ancient shores and which have been preserved, in some cases because of geological uplift, have yielded shell, fish, and shark remains. These do not, however, indicate the presence of a maritime population, as the fish species represented are associated with inshore habitats, and smaller sharks were found on rocky reefs and could have been speared by people lacking even basic fishing-line technology. However, more abundant fish remains from lower levels at the Kilu rock shelter on the island of Buka, at the northern extremity of the Solomon Islands, include some deepwater species ("pelagic," in the scientific literature) such as tuna, which could be caught only offshore.

Jerimalai Cave, in a raised terrace at the eastern extremity of Timor, is especially significant for a substantial assemblage of fish bones, including a high proportion—in the earliest layers of the site—from tuna and a variety of other deepwater species. The remains in question date back to between forty-two thousand and thirty-eight thousand years ago.[18] The finds imply, first, a local population skilled in offshore fishing techniques, which require strong lines and hooks, as well as an understanding of suitable bait or lures. Second, they suggest that the people routinely constructed, over a long period, vessels appropriate to fishing offshore. These were probably dugout canoes that might not have been large (line fishing can be undertaken by just one or two individuals) but would have been well-balanced and seaworthy, given the challenges of bringing in any larger tuna or similar fish. Third, the finds indicate a broader pattern of social life and subsistence that complements this expertise. As the people were not horticulturalists, they would otherwise have hunted and foraged. Any use of stable canoes, as opposed to more improvised temporary watercraft, might imply a semi-settled residence pattern rather than the nomadism usually associated with hunter-gatherer lifestyles. People would surely not have invested the time and energy involved in boat making only to leave vessels behind, unless they were maritime nomads who took their canoes wherever they went.

The Papuan settlement of the Bismarck Islands and the Solomons can hardly be imagined without adaptation to life on water and a developed capacity to produce seaworthy vessels. Indeed, the necessary boats would have been bigger than those that could have taken a couple of men fishing (fishing was, historically, a male rather than a female or mixed activity across Oceania). The passage from the New Guinea mainland across to New Britain could be undertaken while maintaining two-way visibility—that is, both land behind and land ahead were visible. The crossing from New Ireland to Buka (achieved by thirty-two thousand years ago) was either 87 or 109 miles, and the destination would not become visible until the boat was 25 to 34 miles away from the departure point, depending on the specific route. But the settlement of Manus, at the northeastern extremity of the Bismarck Archipelago, was a challenge of an entirely different order. The shortest sea crossing, successfully made by twenty-five thousand years ago, was some 140 miles. For around a third of the voyage, both the land behind and the land ahead would have been out of view. So this was a speculative venture, toward islands that might not have existed, undertaken by people presumably confident in their capacity to explore and return home in the event that they encountered nothing but open water. No comparable or longer open-ocean voyage has been evidenced archaeologically up to this time in history. The seas to the north and east of New Guinea appear to have been realms of human experimentation of an extraordinary and unprecedented kind.[19]

Such discoveries of course raise the question of *why*: Why did people seek to, or need to, colonize new lands? One seemingly obvious response, crowding or population pressure, was clearly not the reason; population densities were low in this epoch. Were people driven, rather, by a spirit of adventure? As Matthew Spriggs, a distinguished archaeologist of Southeast Asia and the Pacific, has reflected, "These kinds of ultimate-cause questions always disturb me, as the glib answers that people often give always reveal more about the self-image or concerns of our age than they do about any past reality." Hence, wanderlust, for example, suggests absurdly that people in the Pleistocene needed to get away from the ancient equivalent of office drudgery.[20]

What can be said is that the longer process exemplifies human initiative. The colonization of Manus notably involved the introduction of wild animals from elsewhere for food (including bandicoots and cuscus, a type of possum), as well as useful plants (such as Canarium, which yields edible nuts), though these translocations may not have taken place until nearer to ten thousand years ago.[21]

Notable evidence of innovation in subsistent societies was found in the New Guinea Highlands. Investigations in the Wahgi Valley from the 1960s revealed drains and related features in swamps dating back to nine thousand years ago. These appear to reflect some basic form of horticulture,

Enhanced image of hunting scene, Leang Bulu' Sipong cave, Sulawesi.

which was overlain by extensive gray clay, associated with widespread clearing. Even the early levels provide evidence for the cultivation of bananas, yam, and taro, plants that have loomed large ever since in the lives of Pacific communities. Pollen samples suggest a relatively sudden loss of forest in the surrounding area, which is strongly indicative of human clearing, presumably for gardening. The nature of early horticulture across Papua and in adjacent islands is yet to be more fully understood, but there is no doubt that diverse forms of tree cropping and the cultivation of root crops were practiced across the region, even if the people did not always constitute fully settled agricultural communities.[22]

The subsequent few thousand years would transform Papuan cultures in the interior of New Guinea and the neighboring islands. Change would be brought about by the dynamism of these communities and—in island Melanesia—by interaction with new arrivals. Archaeological discoveries have brought into view aspects of human history across Sahul during the millennia when, we now know, the region was occupied. But the signs of human presence regarding ways of life and belief are like candles in a living, fertile, and vibrant forest at night. We are lucky to glimpse scenes and moments but have little sense of the social landscapes and stories around them. Notwithstanding the primeval associations of tropical rainforests, we do know that there was nothing static or unvarying in the lives of the Papuan ancestors. To the contrary, the region was distinguished not only by a plethora of local adaptations and the invention of new ways of life on water, but also, it appears, by humanity's first experiments in the daunting business of maritime exploration.

3

MAKING CONNECTIONS

Lapita and Beyond

IN JULY 1997, I WAS FORTUNATE TO SPEND A FEW DAYS AMONG the Paiwan, an Aboriginal people in the south central highlands of Taiwan. I was in the country for typically academic reasons, attending a conference at a Taipei research center, but had been invited by a couple of anthropology students who were undertaking fieldwork in the mountainous interior to visit the village in which they were staying. It was an exhilarating, bewildering, and absurdly short trip: I took a crammed local flight from Taipei, arriving late at night in a dimly lit but frenetically busy local airport. After a long drive in the dark—I had no notion of our route or direction—we entered a village. I was aware of a big church and tin-roofed houses interspersed with gardens. We were welcomed by an elderly female shaman who kept sacred venomous snakes in an alarmingly insecure cage in the middle of her living room. Well into the night, we drank beer and watched her videos of local rituals; as well as being the principal local healer, she was a kind of auto-anthropologist. Early the following morning, in front of an imposing wooden god bearing a double-headed snake, we drank millet wine with the ancestors to mark a harvest ceremony. That evening, I was back at the hectic airport.

Uncannily, the shaman and others I met around the village bore wrist and arm tattoos that were strikingly similar to those I had seen on the bodies of many Polynesians during trips to Samoa, Tahiti, the Marquesas, Hawai'i, and elsewhere. Yet Tahiti was almost seven thousand miles away. On returning to Taipei, I visited a small museum dedicated to the Indigenous cultures of the island.[1] (It stands, as if in humble protest, across the road from the National Palace Museum, an awesome, Louvre-like complex dedicated to traditional art from China.) Here were canoes, architectural forms, figure sculptures, and other works and artifacts that again bore motifs remarkably close to those featured on boats, houses, and ceremonial objects in various parts of the Pacific Islands.

Having been a student of Pacific archaeology, I had been taught that Oceanic cultures could be traced back to the island known historically as Formosa, today as Taiwan. Yet the links were ancient; I had no expectation that I would see them exemplified on the bodies of living people or on recently made artifacts. But my excitement—sparked by cultural affinities between peoples separated by successive migrations over millennia and, in the present, by vast distances—made me a little uncomfortable. In making connections, I felt I was indulging in the kinds of comparisons enthusiastically but arbitrarily made by nineteenth-century philologists. I worried that I had somehow ventured into Fornander-land, the Pacific counterpart to Casaubon's realm of daft speculation.

I ought not to have been concerned. In the succeeding twenty years, the Paiwan, among other Aboriginal peoples of Taiwan, have become increasingly interested in expressing the links between their cultures and those of Oceania. In Guam in 2016, at the Festival of Pacific Arts, there was a substantial delegation from Taiwan, mingling with hundreds of Islanders from across Micronesia, the Solomon Islands, Rapa Nui, and, it seemed, everywhere in between. At dances, concerts, and feasts, the tattoos of Paiwanese and Islanders from elsewhere were seen, compared, and celebrated by their bearers, producing contemporary connections out of ancient ones.

Captain James Cook and Joseph Banks had an inkling of the story behind these links. They reasoned, having compared lists of words from Polynesia, island Southeast Asia, and Madagascar, that the peoples of the Pacific had originated in Asia. From the mid-twentieth century on, this basic inference—essentially a hunch that this was the most likely direction of travel—would be substantiated, enlarged, and made nuanced on the basis of several generations of scholars' research across archaeology, linguistics, and genetics. The upshot has been a rich and textured sense of extraordinary chapters in human history, as well as many questions that remain unanswered.

In 1952, the ethnographer turned archaeologist Edward Gifford led a six-month expedition to New Caledonia, which built on work he had undertaken a few years earlier in Fiji, aiming to address the question of Polynesian origins through a search for sites on larger islands in the south-western Pacific. He was accompanied by a younger archae-ologist, Richard Shutler, and both men's wives. Among the areas they investigated was the Foué Peninsula, on the west coast of the island known as the Grande Terre (distinguish-ing the main landmass from the Loyalties and other smaller islands). They were following up on early twentieth-century reports of pottery finds, and they dedicated just five days to a coastal site that yielded well-preserved ceramics. These ce-ramics became famous for their distinctive dentate-stamped designs, that is, patterns pricked into the clay with some hard and sharp instrument such as a fine comb of shell or bamboo. The pottery shards resembled pieces that Gifford had previously found in Fiji and others had found some de-cades earlier in Tonga. Unlike their predecessors, Gifford and Shutler were able to date samples from the pottery-bearing layers, using the then-novel technique of carbon-14 dating. The analysis revealed that the broken pots were around 2,500 years old. After decades of almost vapid spec-ulation, the human settlement of these archipelagoes could be seen in terms that were precise and historical. Oceania would be as susceptible as the Mediterranean to scholarly research, which might identify populations, their social and economic systems, their movements and interactions, and the patterns of cultural influence over time.[2]

Jack Golson, who later led an important investigation in the New Guinea Highlands, had moved from Cambridge to the University of Auckland in the mid-1950s to establish a program of archaeological research in the south Pacific. He soon followed up the work of Gifford and Shutler, excavating sites on the Isle of Pines, off the southern tip of the Grande Terre of New Caledonia. He corroborated their identification of a ceramic tradition that would be named Lapita, after the site from which Gifford and Shutler had obtained their dates. But while these and succeeding finds were important, what was decisive was Golson's imaginative thesis: that the ceramic finds from across the region, extending all the way from the formidable Melanesian territory of the Grande

Lapita ceramic vessel from the Teouma site.

Terre through the archipelagoes of Fiji into western Polynesia, reflected what he called "a community of culture"— a common tradition and, by implication, a people or set of related peoples.[3]

From one perspective, the observation that artifacts were stylistically related, and the inference that their affinities reflected wider connections among the peoples of a region, might seem unremarkable. But the suggestion that a "community" of related peoples occupied these islands and archipelagoes flew in the face of the harsh juxtaposition between Melanesia and Polynesia that had been fundamental to visions of Oceania since d'Urville's mapping of Pacific populations over a century earlier. His Melanesia-Polynesia division had been grounded in physical difference, above all in skin color; it was explicitly hierarchical, indeed, essentially racist. That division had moreover underpinned Te Rangihiroa's effort to celebrate his Polynesian "Vikings of the sunrise" at the expense of Melanesians, whom the Polynesians had bypassed, not only geographically but through their swift ascent toward civilization. To propose that the Melanesians and Polynesians were ancestrally of one dispersed community was to turn deep-seated classifications and stereotypes on their heads.

As archaeological fieldwork was undertaken farther west and north, Lapita pottery was found in Manus (at the northwestern extremity of the Bismarck Archipelago), around the tip of Papua, across the Solomon Islands, New Caledonia, and Vanuatu, and as far as Fiji, Tonga, and Samoa. Lapita pottery's appearance—and, by implication, the arrival of those who had made the pots—in the Bismarcks seemed sudden: most recently, the dates have been refined to a narrow period from about 1410 to 1290 BC. Though it has been argued that aspects of Lapita culture were generated in situ, the appearance of sites associated with those who may be called Lapita people is generally attributed to migration into the region from island Southeast Asia, and ultimately from Taiwan, where pottery was first in evidence from at least five thousand years ago. Ceramic traditions spread south and southeast into the Philippines, Sulawesi, and Halmahera. Wallacea, already settled for some forty-five thousand to fifty thousand years, thus became a realm of interaction: the new arrivals were distinctive not only for their use of ceramics, but for other artifact genres such as ground-edge stone axes and shell fishhooks and ornaments.[4]

It is important to bear in mind that material-culture assemblages—which are anyway only very selectively represented in the archaeological record—are not the same as languages or social groups. The dissemination of objects does not always parallel the movement of languages or population mix. The patterns of interactions in the past were

Looking toward the Teouma archaeological site, Efate, north Vanuatu.

Landscape near Bourail, New Caledonia.

no doubt deeply complex, involving manifold continuities, intrusions, conflicts, and exchanges.

That said, in this case there happens to be broad cor-relation between the migration of Lapita pottery makers into island Melanesia and the movement of language some 3,500 years ago. Comparative linguistics demonstrates un-ambiguously that the languages of island Melanesia and

Polynesia belong to the Austronesian language family, though there are some exceptions. New Guinea was and is still inhabited primarily by speakers of Papuan languages, and the languages of Aboriginal Australia are similarly non-Austronesian. There are also fuzzy edges: some coastal New Guinea peoples such as Mekeo are Austronesian speakers, but the Baining hunter-gatherers of the interior of New Britain speak a non-Austronesian language. This is not unexpected, given that the Bismarck Archipelago and Solomon Islands formed part of the region settled during the Pleistocene, and the region has seen millennia of interaction since then.

Techniques of historical linguistic reconstruction locate a "homeland" for Austronesian speakers on Taiwan and possibly also the nearby mainland. Hence, the perspectives from language and the archaeological evidence converge. It is likely that the people speaking Austronesian languages moved into the Philippines 5,500 years ago. The great language family then began to break up, diverging into the subgroups ancestral to the historic and modern languages that were ultimately distributed from Madagascar in the west to Rapa Nui in the east. Linguistic studies not only enable scholars to point toward the region of origin of the Oceanic cultures and to map the movements of associated populations, but to use vocabulary to reconstruct the way of life of early Austronesian speakers. The common ancestral vocabulary included words for trees and food plants of major importance: coconuts, breadfruit, taro, and banana among them. The people had domesticated dogs, pigs, and chickens. They had words not only for houses but for houses on stilts, implying a propensity to settle on the shores of lagoons or estuaries, and vocabulary associated with canoes that suggests elaboration and some specialization. There is a word specifically for canoes with outriggers—the modern forms include *waka, vaka, va'a,* and other variants. Other terms refer to splashboards, carved prows or sterns, masts, and sails. Tellingly, there is also a term in the common ancestral language for "expert seafarer." This could simply have referred to someone skilled on the water who would captain a vessel. But in the Oceanic context, virtuosity was generally indissociable from mana (spiritual power) and often from genealogy and ritual status. It is speculative, but the term may well reflect the deep antiquity in the region of a role or an identity of master mariner—in all likelihood a heritable status associated not only with navigational aptitude and knowledge but with particular rites and gods.[5]

Socially, status, rank, and hierarchy were present in Austronesian cultures from the beginning: ancestral terms differentiated senior and junior siblings, and by implication distinguished between those descended from them. Aristocratic societies such as those dominated by the Hawaiian and Tongan monarchs in the historic period are late developments and do not suggest that ancient Austronesian kingdoms on a similar scale existed. However, more localized chiefdoms almost certainly did. Hierarchy may have been present in, and vital to the constitution of, societies that appear small-scale and comparatively egalitarian in their organization. Their structures may have been defined by genealogical principles, by complementary relationships between senior and junior lines, by prescribed ritual obligations, or by a principle of precedence, according to which the status of those who arrived first was somehow fundamental to the social order. It may well be the case that in early Austronesian societies, local chiefs led communities in a political sense but were also essentially priests—living representatives of deities. Yet rank took many forms and evolved endlessly over the course of these societies' histories. Austronesian peoples had much in common, but in another sense they became bewilderingly diverse.[6]

It is equally suggestive that among "house" words is one that appears to refer to a larger, communal structure. Longhouses, men's houses, and sacred houses, often on a dramatic scale, were also a feature of the cultures of "old Melanesia," notably in the Sepik River basin of northeastern New Guinea as well as along New Guinea's south coast. It should also be acknowledged that the elaboration of a house as a symbol of a social group takes many forms worldwide. But tribal houses, meeting houses, chiefs' houses, and other community structures—often incorporating decorated posts, facades, and entryways, sculptures of ancestors or gods, engraved or painted images related to local history or myth, and stone figures and panels—were almost pervasively significant among Pacific peoples at the time of colonial contact. It would be surprising if these expressions and celebrations of society and group identity did not have antecedents among early Austronesian peoples.

The settlement of the Pacific was not just a matter of the physical arrival of people. It also entailed the transformation of natural island environments into places owned and occupied by communities. Islanders inhabited islands in this meaningful sense by naming natural features and localities and making them into places that bore spiritual, cultural, and genealogical identities. Gardens, paths, canoe landing places, and many other features were all elements of this cultured environment, but architecture in particular gave sites form and identity. Edifices were often expressive and dramatic, sat at the center of community life, and spoke to ancestry and history.

Whatever culture and way of life came into being among Formosan people five thousand or so years ago was modified as people moved into Wallacea and beyond. The evidence suggests that the first Austronesian speakers in the region of origin grew grain crops, most likely rice or millet. The archaeological record regarding the adoption of either crop farther south is unclear. There is certainly no evidence that those who became Lapita people grew and consumed any type of grain. Rather, their horticultural systems emphasized tubers such as yams, often grown on mounds, and taro, instantly recognizable for its big, pointed, heart-shaped leaves and widely cultivated for its starchy corm. They also grew tree crops such as coconuts and breadfruit. Subject to local environmental conditions, this suite of trees and plants was important across the Pacific historically, and for many Islanders it remains the stuff of everyday sustenance, together with subsequently introduced plants and foods, such as sweet potato (adopted in the prehistoric period) and the wider range of crops and animals that arrived after European contact. While the extent of Lapita settlements suggests substantial communities, and hence a propensity to intensify agriculture that was unprecedented in the region, some of these plants were likely fostered or cultivated by earlier settlers in Wallacea, New Guinea, and the Bismarcks. Their prominence in Oceanic ways of life thus reflects interaction between the new (the Austronesian speakers) and the old (the Papuans) in regions such as the Bismarck Islands over the initial period of Lapita settlement.

It has also been suggested that the new arrivals adopted from the locals their method of cooking in an earth oven.[7] If this is so, what started out as a borrowed technique has become truly a hallmark of Pacific identity. The oven, now variously known as *lovo* (Fijian), *imu* (Hawaiian), and *hangi* (Maori), was and is used only for special occasions, customarily for large-scale ceremonial feasts. Typically, a broad hollow is excavated and filled with good-sized river stones, if they are available, or other rocks. A substantial fire will in time render these white-hot; when the oven is judged ready, any partially burned logs will be removed, so that the stones alone generate the heat for the duration of the cooking. Whole pigs, often wrapped in banana leaves or other greens, will be placed on the stones, as will root vegetables, and then the whole thing is covered with leaves and earth. After five or six hours, even a large pig will be perfectly and succulently cooked. While there are variations from place to place and in the scale and elaboration of the cooking process—given its wide distribution and the sheer length of its history—this style of cuisine has long been a fundamental part of the ceremonial and festive occasions that are so prominent in, and vital to, public life across Oceania.

While Lapita people certainly kept pigs, dogs, and chickens and invested labor and time in agriculture, they lived near, on, and across water. Though much of the ancestral population on Taiwan—a substantial landmass—must perforce have lived inland, those who took to the sea must have been coast dwellers and had vessels capable of longer journeys. This relationship to the water was no doubt accentuated as the people moved into Wallacea, nothing if not a sea of islands. Both obsidian (volcanic glass) and chert (an exceptionally hard sedimentary quartz stone), used as blades, in hafted knives, and as spear points have been found in archaeological sites, sometimes hundreds of kilometers from their natural sources, pointing to trade that involved either long-distance travel by canoe or networks of interlinked exchange partners. A range of fishhooks indicate specialized approaches to fishing: pearl shell was incorporated into sometimes large iridescent lures, used to seek larger species such as tuna, bonito, and mahi-mahi offshore. Again, this aspect of Lapita culture reflects the antiquity of customary subsistence skills, which are maintained even today in many parts of the Pacific. At the time that I lived in the Marquesas, in the 1980s, young men in more isolated settlements who lacked paid employment would often start their days by taking small outrigger canoes out through heavy surf to fish solo in deep water. They seemed, virtually every day, to succeed in catching a fish—the catches were typically as long as their arms, so one was always enough— which would be shared among families, filleted, and consumed raw, traditionally with sea water, sea salt, or seaweed. Today, modern versions of Hawaiian poke and Tahitian *poisson cru* use lemon juice and other introduced ingredients such as soy sauce. The tourists in Honolulu and Papeete, and now those who eat these dishes globally, are unlikely to have any notion of the thousands of years of fishing tradition that lie behind the snack.

In the light of these continuities, there may be some justification for extrapolating some details of ancient Oceanic life from information about more recent centuries. While the exercise could drift into pure speculation, it is reasonable to assume, for example, that the enormous importance of textiles in the historically documented period reflects a dimension of ancient life that was prominent but does not survive in the archaeological record. The literature of the colonial period and more recent anthropological studies alike draw attention to the quotidian use of cloth, the vital role of wrappings in various ritual settings, the prestige associated with fine fabrics (sometimes adorned with feathers or red ochers associated with sanctity), and the importance of textiles in exchange. The deep significance of the material may be indicated obliquely by some of the designs on Lapita pottery. These include motifs identical to those on bark cloth collected by Cook and others from the eighteenth century onward and motif structures reminiscent of woven fabrics. In addition, alongside food plants, trees used for woven products were a vital part of the flora. This includes pandanus—readily identified by the clusters of aerial roots that help support often seemingly top-heavy trees—and ficus, which mainly provided the bark that was soaked, processed, and beaten into the cloth generically known as tapa.[8]

To return to the observation I made on my visit to the Paiwan, it is intriguing that many of the motifs prominent on both the ceramics that were preserved and the textiles that we know only through historic examples are also those in tattoos. While well-preserved human bodies bearing tattoos are extant from archaeological sites in various parts of the world, notably Siberia, no such bodies have been recovered from Pacific sites; however, the "combs" used to ink the skin—a shell or bone blade cut to form a row of sharp points that was struck rapidly by a small, paddle-like mallet—have been found in a few sites. Similar implements, perhaps even the same implements, must have been used to prick patterns into still-damp pots. *Tatau* was so widespread across not only Oceanic but also Austronesian communities that it must already have been a prominent form of expression and identification among early Austronesian speakers.[9]

If there is much that remains uncertain about Lapita people, there can be no doubt that their culture and economy was not only highly adapted to island environments, but also oriented, from an early date, toward travel and exchange. Life involved wide networks, which at the very least must have enabled particular communities to obtain materials and products that they did not have access to at home. Yet interaction at a distance was rarely for purely utilitarian reasons. Individual accomplishment was probably always associated with formalized friendships, partnerships, or alliances with relatives—albeit those distant in both kin terms and geographically—who might meet for periodic communal gatherings and to exchange valuables. Again, it is unwise to speculate about life thousands of years ago on the basis of practices that were observed in the same regions in the nineteenth or twentieth centuries. Yet the Oceanic context implies that one did not typically form social bonds over considerable distances in order to smooth the way for trade. Rather, trade was undertaken in order to initiate social relationships—indeed, to win and maintain renown.

While the earlier settlers of New Guinea, the Bismarck Islands, and the Solomon Islands were technically and environmentally innovative, they appear to have constituted, over the millennia prior to the Austronesian intrusions into the region, comparatively small social groups made up of a few families or a few dozen individuals. In due course, non-Austronesian Islanders would find their own paths to agricultural and social intensification and generate their own forms of dynamic social interaction, connecting extensive populations through systems of regional trade. But at the time of the arrival of Austronesian peoples in the Bismarcks, their culture was something new, powerful, expansive, and perhaps aggressive.

The most astonishing aspect of the history of the Lapita people is the rapidity of their expansion. Over the last twenty years, sustained archaeological research has led to the identification of more than 230 sites from which Lapita pottery has been recovered, over a swath of archipelagoes and ocean approaching three thousand miles in extent, from New Guinea to Samoa. As the American archaeologist Patrick Kirch has put it, "It is increasingly evident that Lapita represents one of the most rapid population expansions across geographic space known anywhere in world history."[10]

The earliest sites are dated to just over three thousand years before the present. They are in the far west, at the northern extremity of the Bismarck Islands, and in the

Arawe Islands off southern New Britain. The Lapita people's specialized relationship to the sea is evident at this formative stage, in the sense that the sites excavated were settlements of stilt houses built out over shallow lagoons. Just
a couple of hundred years later, Lapita people had moved
swiftly south and east, through and beyond the large islands
in the Solomon Archipelago, which are relatively close together and had been occupied for tens of thousands of years.
Across the Solomons, the Lapita Austronesian speakers and
earlier settlers must have been present at the same time and
must have interacted. Whether these relationships were
hostile or more cordial is impossible to know. Certainly over
time these populations mixed. But when the Austronesians
moved farther into the south Pacific, they moved beyond
the limits of earlier human settlement, into the Santa
Cruz Islands, northern Vanuatu, the Loyalty Islands, New
Caledonia, and beyond to Fiji and western Polynesia. They
also ventured north into parts of Micronesia, probably over
a period of not much more than two hundred years: some
dates are as early as those for the Bismarcks, and there are
numerous dates between 2,500 and 3,000 years ago.

These were voyages of discovery over far greater distances than those undertaken earlier. Reaching the Fijian
Islands involved a passage of some 530 miles across open
ocean, farther than the crossings made during the Pleistocene or in any other part of the world in that period. It
is arresting that the project of voyaging was undertaken in
such a sustained manner. It entailed not the establishment
of a new colony followed by a period of growth and consoli-
dation, but an apparent pattern of establishment and swift

onward movement. This is not to say that a single group of voyagers found land and "camped" for a period before moving on. Full-scale settlements were founded; initially small populations evidently grew. But then a subgroup would take to the sea, bringing with them plants, breeding pairs of pigs, dogs, and chickens, and sufficient food and water to survive the next extended passage. They would then reach lands previously unoccupied by any people to establish new settlements and communities, out of which voyaging parties would again venture beyond the world that they knew.

The question of what motivated voyages that were exceptionally arduous and risky is very hard to answer without retrospectively attributing our contemporary sense of human interest and identity to people in the past. Yet, more cautiously, it can be suggested that social values loomed large. Austronesian cultures seem to have privileged the "founders" of particular communities. Those seeking renown might thus understand a successful voyage of colonization, and the foundation of a community, as the ultimate human achievement. Yet it is still hard to understand quite why this culture drove such an extraordinary succession of colonizing ventures at the time that it did. We may also wonder why these took the form of extended sea passages, rather than short-distance, local moves into the abundance of new territory offered across extensive landmasses. New Caledonia's Grande Terre is bigger than the state of Connecticut and more than three-quarters the size of Wales. The archipelago is made up of more than eighty islands—now forming the modern nation of Vanuatu—many of which offered

Pandanus plants near shoreline, Kwamera, Tanna, Vanuatu.

room enough, one might have thought, for new founders and communities.

The Lapita people's colonizing burst began suddenly and came to an end that was not necessarily sudden, but definite. Once they reached Fiji and western Polynesia, they settled the wide range of larger and smaller islands, from Viti Levu through the Tongan archipelago to Upolo and Savai'i. They reached this region around 1000 BC, but communities and culture then developed across these relatively proximate island groups for nearly two thousand years before venturing farther.

This was the environment in which Polynesian culture assumed a distinct identity. "Polynesia," as we saw earlier, was one of Jules-Sébastien-César Dumont d'Urville's terms, an invention of nineteenth-century racial anthropology that was juxtaposed negatively with "Melanesia" for well over a century. But the fact that d'Urville's theorization was an expression of its time—indeed, of invidious

Kava-drinking house (nakamal), Kwamera, Tanna, Vanuatu.

colonial thought—did not mean that it was entirely wrong. Whereas the French geographer's other two regional and ethnic types—Melanesian and Micronesian—did not reflect ancestrally unified cultures or coherent traditions (let alone "races"), there were and are Polynesian peoples, cultures, and languages that have common origins.

"Polynesia" began with the Lapita's furthest movement east.[11] Fiji was settled very soon after New Caledonia and the Solomons, between 1100 and 1000 BC; people appear to have moved on to Tonga and Samoa by 900 to 850 BC. In the same way that the dispersed Lapita peoples had constituted, as Jack Golson proposed, a "community of culture," an ancestral Polynesian culture likewise constituted a distributed "community"—albeit one later in its formation and that occupied a more limited geographic realm. That theater of settlement and interaction for these ancestors of the Polynesians included the Tongan and Samoan archipelagoes and the smaller islands of 'Uvea, Futuna, and Niue. Those islands are dispersed across seas that are comparatively extensive: it is 370 miles from the northern islands of the Tongan archipelago to Savai'i and Upolu, the largest of the Samoan Islands. That distance raises the question of what "community" could have meant for the peoples who occupied these islands. Those who assume that Indigenous cultures were generally localized might imagine that on each island were communities with particular identities and traditions, leading separate lives. No doubt each local group did have its own story and sense of belonging. But the seas were realms of interaction, across which people maintained relationships and affinities. The innovations that marked these societies' development were broadly shared. The Lapita settlers of the region became different from other Lapita peoples to the west, who had their own histories, and in this way the ancestors of the Polynesians became distinctive together, inventing new institutions, beliefs, and practices. They would become the peoples whom outsiders from Europe would recognize as a singular nation, as the Europeans encountered the cultures of eastern Oceania from the eighteenth century onward.

Ancestral Polynesian cultures shared and refined the horticultural practices of their Lapita ancestors, growing root crops, such as taro and yams, and cultivating breadfruit, coconuts, bananas, plantains. They also grew pandanus, from which mats were woven, and ficus species for the bark used to make tapa cloth. Extended families constituted descent groups, which together made up a tribe. Such tribes traced their ancestry back to an individual founder; those identified as the first-born descendants of that founder were chiefs, generally known as *tui, ariki*, or some cognate term. Chiefs may have enjoyed some nominal or titular ownership of the group's lands and acted as the priests, making offerings of first fruits to ancestral gods. Yet while nineteenth-century European observers saw Polynesian societies in terms of their own historical, political models, and often referred to local leaders as "kings," Polynesian political formations were in fact fluid, embracing shifting statuses. Chiefs, priests, warriors, and shamans were in competition; alliances might enable particular aristocrats and families to gain an ascendancy previously enjoyed by a different group. In addition, expert sailors, tattooists, artists, and healers

ST. JOHN THE BAPTIST PARISH LIBRARY
2920 NEW HIGHWAY 51
LAPLACE, LOUISIANA 70068

were like specialized priests, with particular status of their own. Hierarchy was not fixed, and genealogy more a realm of contest than an order establishing enduring relationships of rank. Concepts of *tapu* (anglicized as "taboo" following Cook's voyages) reflected complex understandings of sanctity and power rather than a simple religious prohibition. Mana (spiritual power) was similarly a vital notion across Polynesia, and it had deeper roots, as it was prominent, too, across Melanesia in the historic period.

Long-distance trade was significant throughout Oceania's history. In Polynesia, trade continued and large-scale ceremonial exchange assumed greater importance. As has been previously acknowledged, it may be methodologically dubious to extrapolate back to earlier periods from practices documented among Polynesians of the historic period. Yet in western Polynesia particularly, it is notable that social groups always regularly engaged in large-scale offerings of food and valuables to kin, and in particular with people with whom intermarriage took place. Society was in this sense inherently extra-local: A group would periodically venture elsewhere to make substantial presentations and to be recipients of feasts or other offerings. The staging of such transactions would entail rituals of arrival and welcome, oratory, performance, and dance. Gift giving was typically also competitive: donors would aim to be extravagant, the scale of their gifts an expression of their strength and mana.

Reconstruction can go only so far, but there are a few things we can know with confidence. It is certain that tattoo, chieftainship, genealogy, and some subsistence practices formed part of an ancestral Polynesian culture. It is also very likely that more specific cultural formations, such as rituals associated with first fruits and beliefs associated with *tapu*, sanctity, and cloth—which frequently wrapped or "contained" sacredness—similarly became significant in the cultures of western Polynesia more than two thousand years ago. It can also be suggested that the canoe-building, navigational, and sailing skills, which were no doubt already formidable, were further refined over these centuries. The "community of culture" among which Polynesian identity took shape was an interisland community: connected not by the occupation of a shared territory, but by paths across water.

If the reasons for the Lapita's extraordinary expansion, and that expansion's pause in western Polynesia, are ultimately mysterious, so are the factors that prompted Polynesians to adventure and voyage farther. For whatever reason, just over a thousand years ago a new set of expeditions took place, taking Polynesians to a wide range of archipelagoes and islands right across the Pacific. While theorists had previously envisaged one phase of settlement in the Marquesas and a set of further voyages from there, it now appears that central-eastern Polynesia island groups—including the Cook Islands, the Society Islands, Mangareva, and the Marquesas—were first occupied around 900 AD. The Norwegian adventurer Thor Heyerdahl argued for decades in support of the thesis that Indigenous South Americans voyaged into the Pacific. However, Kirch and other archaeologists consider the evidence for limited American-Polynesian interaction—most notably the presence of sweet potato from the continent in eastern Polynesia—as most

plausibly interpreted as taking place through Polynesian return voyages, perhaps even just one return voyage, from
the islands to the South American coast.[12]

It is notable that the extensive islands of the Tuamotus,
which constitute the largest atoll archipelago in the world,
were also settled early. Like the islands of Kiribati, the Marshall Islands, and other Micronesian archipelagoes, this
chain of some eighty islands offered first settlers extremely
challenging environments. Atolls are typically narrow, broken rings of dry land, just a couple of meters above sea level,
separating often vast lagoons from deep open ocean. There
is no stone other than coral, soils are sandy and highly sa-
line, there are no streams, the natural flora is exceptionally
impoverished, bird species are not numerous, and there are
no land animals other than those introduced deliberately
or inadvertently by people. Some breadfruit varieties can
be grown, as their roots reach a subsurface freshwater lens
(a layer of groundwater deriving from rainfall), and some
atoll dwellers dug pits that extended into this lens in order to cultivate giant taro. In addition to these plants, the
coconut palms and pandanus that grew on the atolls were
vital to human life. Coconuts provided nutritious milk and
meat, and the nuts and leaves of pandanus were edible.
Both palms and pandanus provided essential raw materials
for woven mats and baskets, sails, fiber for fishing lines and
nets, materials for house building, and much else. Early settlers used various types of shell to make implements that
elsewhere were made of stone—adzes made from giant
clams, for example—and personal ornaments were likewise
cut from shells and sometimes the spines of sea urchins.

Archaeologists refer frequently to human adaptation to environments. In the case of the people who arrived on these atolls—presumably from very different, environmentally diverse high islands like Tahiti—something more than adaptation was necessary: they embraced a larger and more extraordinary reinvention of subsistence and life. Yet it was also a mode of life that remained extra-local. At the time of Cook's voyages, Tahitians certainly made canoe voyages to the Tuamotus to obtain products such as pearl shell. Johann Forster noted that the "low islanders" had dogs with distinctively long, white fur, which was sought after in the Society Islands. Referring to paper mulberry (*Broussonetia papyrifera*), the tree whose bark was most commonly used for cloth, he noted that the atoll dwellers were unable to "cultivate the mulberry-tree on their sandy, barren ledges of lands." These "reciprocal wants," then, stimulated "a kind of commerce between the inhabitants of the high and low islands."[13]

Further archaeological research will inevitably refine dates for first settlement across the region, but it appears that the Austral Islands, Hawai'i, and Rapa Nui were reached by about 1100 AD, and New Zealand a century or so later. These dates—many from dune sites close to beaches—suggest rapid expansion over the course of relatively few generations, much like the swift succession of earlier Lapita expeditions. It is remarkable but probable that someone of the time might have arrived on one island as an infant and then seen children and grandchildren embark—from what had become an established community during his or her lifetime—on voyages to seek further islands and establish new communities.

Yet, despite the apparent rapidity of this expansion, the particular traits associated with eastern Polynesia do imply the development of an identity distinct from that of the western Polynesian societies. These traits are recognizable in material culture, in distinctive kinds of tanged adze blades (implying an interest in sophisticated woodworking) and in an elaborate diversity of fishhooks. There is also an unambiguously clear linguistic cluster of eastern Polynesian dialects—hence the ease with which the Society Islander Tupaia communicated with Maori when he accompanied Cook on the *Endeavour* to New Zealand. The strictly linguistic evidence suggests that there are two main ancestral eastern Polynesian languages: one from which Tahitian, Tuamotuan, Maori, and various Cook Islands languages derive, and the other ancestral to Marquesan, Hawaiian, and Mangarevan. Rapanui, on its own, constitutes a third, distinct category.

There are equally notable shared eastern Polynesian cultural forms in the development of marae (temples and associated precincts), which sometimes feature stepped platforms or vertical stones representing deified ancestors (in the Tuamotus, equivalents are made from coral rock). There are also overlaps in a range of more specific beliefs and protocols, from those around *tapu* to understandings of the afterlife. An eastern Polynesian homeland cannot have been occupied for long before voyagers moved on to more distant islands. A period of two-way voyaging likely also sustained common cultural development. Subsequently, however, it appears that as the populations of archipelagoes grew, social relations and interactions came to be played out within rather than between island groups, and longer-distance, inter-archipelagic voyaging became less frequent for peoples such as the Marquesans and Hawaiians.

The relative homogeneity of eastern Polynesian culture is striking, and it was the observation of affinities from Rapa Nui to Aotearoa (New Zealand) that enabled, or compelled, Cook and his companions to recognize that a single "great nation" had dispersed itself across the vast ocean. However, at another level, the diversity of local social, political, and cultural development from Tahiti to the Marquesas, and from

Sataua, Upolu, Samoa, 1982.

the Hawaiian Islands to New Zealand, is impressive. Across these related cultures, there were indeed cognate expressions of chieftainship and monarchy, but it is notable that in Hawai'i a class-stratified, island-wide kingdom emerged. This system had the capacity to mobilize commoner labor to construct major temple sites and resource-management systems, such as large-scale taro pond fields and extensive lagoon fish reserves involving stone walls and weirs.[14] This system was very different from the comparatively decentralized political forms that emerged in the Marquesas and among New Zealand Maori. Notwithstanding the development of different kinds of intensive agriculture (the Marquesans focused particularly on breadfruit, which was preserved in a fermented form in pits), chiefs typically had limited power and were engaged in ongoing albeit small-scale warfare. They were also responsible for the staging of feasts that periodically brought allied groups from across islands and territories together. In Polynesia, political transformation evidently entailed both evolution (the development of more centralized and stratified formations) and what may be seen as devolution (a move from what may have been more coherent ancestral chiefdoms toward local-level political leadership).

The latter developments were marked in eastern Polynesia by opportunistic patterns of alliance. Men and women of chiefly lineage would claim power, supported (or not) by warriors and shamans. Their success was dependent on shifting groups of local followers and on sheer performance in warfare and ceremonial life, as opposed to any kind of more enduring order. Among the most famous expressions of such devolution was the competitive birdman cult among Rapanui, most likely a sixteenth- or seventeenth-century development that superseded a more traditional hierarchy around the paramount chiefs—represented in the iconic *moai*, the great stone ancestor figures—who were displaced over a period of intensified local conflict. Sometimes sensationalized in films and other accounts of Rapanui life, this social upheaval has frequently been taken out of its proper context. Indeed, it is typical of popular representation of Oceania that cultural forms are treated as spectacular and unique, rather than as expressions of dynamic tendencies that were widely present in life in the Pacific. Local religion, for example, was never static: new cults emerged to displace older beliefs regularly in many island milieus. Chiefs and dynasties were similarly prone to suffer rejection, espccially if they failed to maintain the prosperity they ideally provided their people. Among European travelers in the Pacific, the more perceptive always recognized that the societies they encountered were not unchanging customary regimes, but more like the places they themselves came from: realms of conflict and invention, in politics as well as belief.

The diversification of art in eastern Polynesia over the centuries of separate cultural development among Cook Islanders, Maori, Marquesans, Tahitians, and Hawaiians is also remarkable—and readily recognizable, if you have the chance to walk around the Oceania galleries in museums of world culture.[15] Of course, there are notable underlying affinities, and images of deities and ancestors in wood and stone were prominent across all these cultures. Yet the sophistication, coherence, resolution, and distinctiveness of varied design and motif systems, especially among Maori and Marquesans, is astonishing. In each art tradition, there is an entire visual language of involuted designs: prominently curvilinear in the Maori case, and constituted out of square forms with rounded, interlocking transitions in the Marquesas. The artists engraved such motifs around the bodies of sculpted ancestors and a whole variety of vessels, implements, and weapons alike. Similar designs in *tatau* wrapped the bodies of men and women. Yet nothing was standardized: some genres bore plain surfaces, and were compelling in form, rather than through decoration. The great German ethnographer of the Marquesas, Karl von den Steinen, thought that *'u'u* clubs—which featured multiple faces within faces, as well as apparently abstract motifs—could only have been refined over many centuries, yet they may in fact have been a very late artistic innovation. On the *Endeavour*, Joseph Banks had been entranced by Maori sculpture, and he had his artists produce minutely careful illustrations of canoe prows among other forms. Of one style he wrote, "I may truly say was like nothing but itself."[16]

Yet these wonderfully distinctive art styles did have common origins among groups ancestral to Maori, Marquesans, Society Islanders, and others. Among very few surviving early sculptures is the piece known as the Kaitaia carving.[17] In 1920, this magnificent work was discovered during the construction of a drainage system in a swamp outside the town of Kaitaia, in the north of New Zealand's North Island. The find was later dated to the fourteenth century and thus determined to have been made by Maori ancestors, within just a hundred or so years of their first settlement. Over two

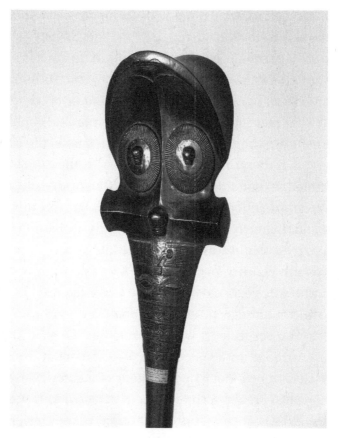

'U'u, war club, Marquesas Islands, late eighteenth or early nineteenth century.

meters wide, the sculpture is generally supposed to have
formed the central, overhead part of a gateway, most likely
to some sort of temple. It features an angular, squat central figure with outstretched arms, linked with elongated
arcs that connect with what may be the tails of abstract but
lizard-like predatory figures with extended jaws. The Kaitaia
carving is dissimilar to the Maori art of the historic period,

111

yet it has been much remarked on for its close affinities with pieces from the Austral Islands and Society Islands. Since 1931, ethnologists have pointed to its similarity to a sculpture in the Museum of Archaeology and Anthropology in Cambridge, which is evidently a fragment of something larger. That piece features two anthropomorphic double figures that are as squat and angular as the one on the Kaitaia carving, and the arm of one is linked with the tail of some quadruped, either a dog or a pig. The Cambridge piece was collected during Cook's first voyage, but it has recently been dated and seems to have been an antiquity at that time. The dates suggest that it was made in the late sixteenth or early seventeenth century, meaning that it was probably between fifty and eighty years old at the time Cook acquired it.

The Cambridge piece was, moreover, long misrecognized in two respects. It was described in the scholarly literature, without evidence, as a "canoe ornament," but it is more likely to be a detached element of a gateway carving, perhaps one end of a form like the Kaitaia work. It was also understandably attributed to the Austral Islands, given that Australs sculpture often featured angular forms and the zigzags or chevrons, also present in the openwork element of

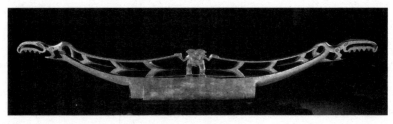

Tangonge, the Kaitaia carving, AD 1300–1400.

Sculpture of two double figures and a quadruped, Tahiti, c. 1690–1730.

the Kaitaia form. In fact, wood-isotope analysis has demonstrated that the work was from Tahiti or elsewhere in the
Society Islands. Given the brevity of the *Endeavour*'s contacts with Austral Islanders (at Rurutu), it was never likely
that the artifact was obtained there, though it could conceivably have been made in Rurutu but traded to Tahiti prior to
being given to or bartered with Cook or some other member
of the expedition.

In any case, the resemblances between the two sculptures pointed toward the ancestral connections between
Maori and the peoples of central-eastern Polynesia. There is
no suggestion that the Kaitaia work was directly influenced
by the Tahitian piece, not least because the latter was made
three hundred to four hundred years after the former. But
the two works undoubtedly reflect a deeper, shared artistic
heritage. Some ninety years after their similarities had been
noted in the pages of the *Journal of the Polynesian Society*,

they were exhibited together for the first time in 2018, in the "Oceania" exhibition at the Royal Academy in London.[18] Among those present at the exhibition opening and ritual blessing were senior members of Te Runanga-o-te-Rarawa (the tribal council associated with the Kaitaia carving's place of discovery) and representatives from Tahiti. The descendants of the makers of both carvings mingled, expressing admiration and wonder before these extraordinary and expressively similar works of their ancestors.

4

"THE BEST OF ANY BOATS
IN THE WORLD"

O<small>N</small> M<small>AY</small> 21, 1686, <small>THE</small> *C<small>YGNET</small>* <small>CAME TO ANCHOR OFF</small> G<small>UAM'S</small> western coast, following a grueling passage from Mexico— provisions were all but exhausted. The buccaneer and writer William Dampier would have less than two weeks to observe Chamorro life, but he was profoundly impressed, in particular, by their voyaging canoes, and he described them carefully:

> The Natives are very ingenious beyond any people, in making Boats, or Proes, as they are called in the *East-Indies*, and therein they take great delight. These are built sharp at both ends; the bottom is of one piece, made like the bottom of a little Canoa, very neatly dug, and left of a good substance. This bottom part is instead of a Keel. It is about 26 or 28 foot long; the under part of this Keel is made round, but inclining to a wedge, and smooth; and the upper part is almost flat,

Steering oar, Kairiru Island, Papua New Guinea, late nineteenth century.

having a very gentle hollow, and is about a foot broad: From hence both sides of the boat are carried up to about 5 foot high with narrow Plank, not above 4 or 5 inches broad, and each end of the Boat turns up round, very prettily.[1]

Dampier proceeded to describe "the little boat"—that is, the outrigger—"to keep the great Boat upright from over-setting." He went on to explain how these vessels, having no differentiated prow or stern, could change direction in the wind without tacking "only by shifting the end of the yard." "I have been more particular" in describing the canoes, Damp-ier wrote, "because I do believe, they sail the best of any Boats in the World." The people were, he affirmed, "no less dextrous in managing, than in building" them. He believed they were able to undertake return voyages to neighboring islands thirty leagues (about 104 miles) away within twelve or so hours, and to sail to Manila in four days.[2]

The sailing canoes of the Chamorro were the creations of people who had settled western Micronesia from the Philippines, rather than descendants of Lapita voyagers. By the time Dampier described these vessels, they may well have been refined, following renewed contacts with island Southeast Asia. Their antecedents—along with seagoing canoes throughout the Pacific—were made without metal tools of any kind, but it would be surprising if the makers of the boats Dampier observed had not obtained iron from

Mauke, Cook Islands, 1982.

the Spanish. Iron-bladed adzes and knives would have made the vast amount of woodworking that went into these boats swifter and easier, though neither the perfection of the canoes' architecture nor their materials are likely to have been modified as a result of European contact, since the design principles of the Oceanic vessels were fundamentally different from those of European ships (which owed their stability to their squat cross section, weight, and ballast).

Most of the Europeans who encountered Islanders over the early period of cross-cultural contact were, like Dampier, professional mariners who knew ships and their management intimately. They were predisposed to be interested in Islanders' craft, and the best observers among them described the canoes, their rigs, and their sailing capacities minutely. In some places, local boats were considered to be of indifferent quality. This was said, for example, at Rapa Nui, where a shortage of timber meant that the best people could do was produce small canoes for fishing near shore. Around the shores of most islands, the great majority of canoes sighted were similarly appropriate for lagoon or offshore fishing, rather than for any extended passage. But early visitors were full of admiration for the larger vessels they saw and had the opportunity to observe under sail.

Among the first accounts were those of the Dutch navigators Jacob Le Maire and Willem Schouten, who approached islands in the north of the Tongan archipelago in April 1616. They saw a sail that they at first thought was Spanish, and they tried to bear down upon what, it soon became evident, was not a European ship but a "bark." The

Engraving from Schouten depicting the 1616 Dutch attack on a Tongan canoe.

occupants of the canoe were alarmed and sought to avoid the Dutch, while the Dutch, for their part, fired upon the canoe repeatedly, ostensibly not wishing to harm anyone but with the intention of forcing the other crew to strike their sails and come alongside. A number of the Islanders jumped overboard and threw valuables such as mats and chickens into the water. Though some among the Islanders drowned, the Europeans provided assistance to others, treating the injuries of one man who was shot, exchanging some articles, and eventually permitting them to continue on their way.[3]

The vessel they had encountered was not only a double canoe of some size, but evidently one engaged in a longer-distance voyage, possibly even a voyage of settlement. The Dutch estimated there were about twenty-five people on board, including babies, young children, women, and at least one older man; they had coconuts with them, but relatively few, and they appeared to be drinking sea water.

> Their bark was of a wonderful constructure and of strange figure. . . . It was made of two long and handsome canoes, between which there was a good space, about the middle of them were two planks, very broad, of red wood, raised on their edges, and across upon them some small beams, and above these other planks, the whole very close, compact, and well made fast the one on the other; towards the fore part of one canoe, on the starboard side, it had a forked stick, serving for a mast, on which their sail, made of matts and of the same shape as those used by Spanish barks, was stuck; they were very proper and well fitted for sea; they had neither compass, nor other sea instrument, but only hooks for fishing, of which the upper parts were of stone, and the lower of some black bones or of tortoise-shell, some were also of mother of pearl. Their cables were very thick, and extremely well made of a stuff almost of the same appearance as are made the matts for packing Spanish figs: when they left us they made their course toward the S E.[4]

Among remarks of interest in this account is the reference to "red wood," which was almost certainly *fehi* or *Intsia bijuga*, an Indo-Pacific teak that could grow to more than 150 feet in height and yielded a hard, insect-resistant timber. It was not only for these qualities, however, that it was sought after by canoe builders of the region. *Calophyllum, Dysoxylum* (commonly known as rosewoods), and *Terminalia richii* (*malili* in Samoan) were also large trees highly appropriate for the construction of canoes. What was distinctive about *fehi* was its dark red sap. Red was a *tapu* color, associated with power, sanctity, and high chiefly status throughout Oceania. The double canoe encountered by the Dutch was probably owned by an aristocratic family, and some among those who were unceremoniously shot at by the Europeans were in all likelihood of high rank. The

A boy with a harpoon standing on the bow platform of a double canoe, Mawatta, Papua New Guinea, 1910–12.

Palms and shore, Kwamera, Tanna, Vanuatu.

Europeans were powerfully impressed by the double canoe, but they had no way of understanding that it was not just an expression of maritime technology but also one of great social status and spiritual power.

It is also intriguing that the Islanders were said to have "made their course" on departure toward the southeast. If this is right, they were not heading toward the closest, larger islands of the Samoan group, nor in the direction of any part of the Tongan archipelago to the southwest. Rather, possibly, they could have been going toward Niue, some three hundred miles southeast, or potentially much farther, toward Rarotonga or others of the Cook Islands, more than three times that distance. Soon afterward, off the high island of

Niuatoputapu, Le Maire and Schouten encountered further Tongans and saw more double canoes, one of which at least was so large that it carried a smaller boat:

> These people had also in their ship a canoe which they could put into the water when occasion required, and are very good mariners; their ships were of the same figure as those above-mentioned; they are very well fitted with sails, and run so well under sail, that there are very few ships in Holland which could beat them.[5]

A canoe returns from the main island of Malakula to Atchin, decorated for a ceremony, paddled by men dressed for dance. Photograph by the anthropologist John Layard, 1914.

The first of the "barks" sighted was depicted in an engraving, the earliest image published in Europe of any Oceanic vessel. Though no original drawing exists, the printed version appears, somewhat unusually for the period, to reproduce carefully whatever sketch was made at the time: the structure of the vessel and the form of the mast and the rig, as well as the figure of a chicken on the pandanus sail—all are essentially consistent with later representations of similar double canoes. In this case, the rig was of the *tongiaki* type, with fixed stays that limited the versatility of the vessel. This has been considered a primitive system relative to the *kalia* rig with a canting mast, which could be repositioned in the manner described by Dampier. Over the course of the eighteenth and early nineteenth centuries, these rigs were modified, hybridized, and adapted by Tongans, Fijians, and others in the region.[6]

More extensive observations of canoes were made during Cook's voyages, especially during his second voyage, of 1772 to 1775, when his crews encountered an unprecedented range of peoples across the Pacific. Again in the Tongan archipelago, George Forster made detailed observations of ingenious aspects of canoe construction. Whereas the Tahitian method of sewing planks together made the boats leaky, he noted that the Tongans (and Fijians and others) shaped the edges of each plank "in such a manner as to leave a projecting lift or rim close to the edge, and through this they pass their threads," thus enabling the stitching to be wholly internal to the hull. Writing of relatively smaller fishing canoes, he stated that although the boats were "commonly fifteen to eighteen feet long, yet they are as neatly and smoothly polished as our best cabinet-work, which must appear the more surprising when we consider that the tools of the natives are only wretched bits of coral, and rasps made of the skin of rays."[7]

This was overstated: Islander woodworking tools included finely polished and sharpened basalt adzes, though shark and stingray skins were indeed used in a similar manner to sandpaper. But the broader point, that the work was consummately executed, was certainly fair. While less care may have been taken with smaller fishing canoes, larger vessels exemplified the prestige of the groups, the chiefs who led them, their affluence, and their spiritual power.

Forster also noted that some larger canoes could carry as many as 150 men. He also corroborated the Dutch observation, noting that the sails "are made of strong mats, in which the rude figure of a tortoise or a cock, &c. is sometimes represented." Cook himself was profoundly impressed with the Tongan vessels, remarking that they were "fit for distant navigation." He implied that the Islanders were as capable as European mariners, whose voyages over great distances had been accomplished only in recent centuries from the perspective of his own time.

In August and September 1777, during his third voyage, Cook returned to Tahiti for another extended visit. On his departure he knew he would not return, and his parting from the high chiefs and others he had visited over a period of eight years was emotional. One of the preeminent chiefs, Tu (also known as Pōmare I), presented him with a sixteen-foot double canoe, a large model of the grandest type of vessel, which was apparently built specifically as a present for

Cook—or, rather, as a gift to be conveyed to King George III. It featured extensive sculpted decoration.[8] Unfortunately, Cook considered the va'a too large to transport; had it ended up in a northern-hemisphere museum, an early Tahitian canoe would be extant. As it is, interested Polynesians and scholars have only illustrations to go on, though some of the drawings made in the field are, so far as we can tell, careful and accurate. John Webber, the artist on the third voyage, made a fine sketch of a double canoe at around this time, which appears to be about the size mentioned; it may well depict the gift Cook felt obliged to decline.

Although many museums hold model canoes from various parts of the Pacific (mainly souvenirs made in the late nineteenth century and subsequently) and despite the presence of wonderful examples of river, lagoon, and smaller fishing canoes in a number of collections, there are unfortunately very few historic vessels that were used for open-ocean voyages. Exceptions include the Fijian drua, of which huge examples were made late in the nineteenth century, and which are well documented through precise drawings and colonial-era photographs. There is a complete, smaller example in the Fiji Museum, which, together with documentary sources, has enabled craftsmen to revive the form, adhering faithfully to traditional materials and design.

Perhaps the most remarkable oceangoing canoe in any museum is one from Luf, the largest of a group of small islands known as the Hermit Islands, west of Manus. Though in a geographic sense the cluster is a westward extension of the Bismarck Islands, Luf—together with Wuvulu and Aua—is sometimes said to belong to a cultural province

Outrigger voyaging canoe from Luf, on display in the Ethnologisches Museum, Berlin.

awkwardly termed "para-Micronesia." These islands—much closer to the New Guinea mainland than any archipelago conventionally considered part of Micronesia—were thought to have strong cultural affiliations with the atoll cultures farther north. The German ethnologist Georg Thilenius visited Luf briefly in the course of the 1908–1910 Südsee-Expedition (a major scientific voyage to German-administered territories in Micronesia and Melanesia) and saw a remarkable canoe on a beach there, but curiously he was unable to take the time to study it. However, Maximilian

Thiel, a German trader who actively sought and trafficked in ethnographic artifacts, went to considerable trouble to have the richly decorated outrigger canoe transported to his main station at Matupit, at the northern end of New Britain. The Danish ethnographer Richard Parkinson was able to photograph it in the water while it was there. Thiel in due course sold it to the Museum für Völkerkunde in Berlin.[9]

Navukinivanua, a Fijian outrigger voyaging canoe, with many prominent Fijian chiefs on board, c. 1877.

Local model of a Fijian *ndrua*, double-hulled canoe with a pandanus mat sail, collected 1875–77.

The fifty-two-foot Luf boat is quite unlike most documented Oceanic canoes. Its hull forms a deep V, its sides are nearly vertical, and an area of decking between the main vessel and the outrigger supports a large timber chest, perhaps for storing food or for transporting trade goods. Two masts bear large rectangular sails of broad woven fiber. The prow and stern feature high, circular forms, abundantly decorated with fiber tassels. Strikingly, the entire hull is painted with interlocking curvilinear motifs, giving the canoe an animated, energetic appearance. Near the prow, the apparently abstract motifs give way to a visual surprise in the form of a pair of human figures. Those who have the chance to look closely at this amazing canoe cannot but be astonished by the intricacy of the sinnet (coconut-fiber) bindings and lashings that hold the whole vessel together and the beauty of the sculpted and decorated oars, among many other aspects of the vessel and its accoutrements.

The abundance of what are, in effect, testimonials to Pacific seacraft, along with the actual specimens of a few great vessels, would seem to be a vindication of the capacity of Islanders to construct and sail canoes over the vast distances entailed by the settlement of eastern Polynesia, in particular. But mid-twentieth-century scholars reacted against the overt romanticism of writers such as Te Rangi-hiroa. In particular, the New Zealand historian Andrew Sharp (1906–1974), a Rhodes scholar and distinguished civil servant, generated intense controversy when he published *Ancient Voyagers in the Pacific* in 1956. The book, initially brought out by the Polynesian Society, secured a global readership through a London printing as a Pelican paperback a year later.[10] The core of Sharp's argument was that Islanders did not have the capacity to sail beyond approximately three hundred miles. Therefore, all the more remote Oceanic islands must have been settled accidentally, by those undertaking more localized passages who had got lost, were caught in storms, or had otherwise drifted, unintentionally arriving at new island homes. As Jack Golson noted some twenty years later, the book generated heated debate, especially in New Zealand, but also among scholars internationally: "It is difficult to convey the extent of the controversy . . . in scholarly journals, the popular press, public lectures and private discussions, and the depth of feeling that was aroused."[11] This in part because, just as Rangihiroa's *Vikings of the Sunrise* reflected great pride in the achievements of Polynesian voyagers, Sharp's arguments conversely appeared to cast aspersions and diminish the skills and accomplishments of Islanders.

It has been widely acknowledged that this provocation was of decisive importance in motivating a range of experimental studies. These included early computer simulations, which sought to establish how likely drift voyages from starting points in eastern Polynesia were to arrive in the Hawaiian archipelago, and the reconstruction of historical Polynesian canoes that were employed in reenactment voyages intended to demonstrate that traditional navigational techniques would enable long-distance expeditions.[12]

Sharp's thesis suffered from obvious drawbacks. Across Oceania, deep-sea fishing is an activity strongly identified with men, as is warfare. Were fishermen or warriors to have been carried away, unable to sail home, but sufficiently fortunate to drift to a new land, a lack of women would have precluded the emergence of a new population. Mixed-sex groups were found on canoes mainly when people traveled for festive or diplomatic purposes. In some archipelagoes, such trips were undertaken periodically, but it is hard to see how or why many such interisland passages should suffer the misfortune to be thrown off course.

More fundamentally, Islanders across the Pacific practiced horticulture with a similar range of food plants and kept pigs, dogs, and chickens. While those undertaking shorter voyages to visit kin might conceivably have taken gifts of live animals with them, perhaps fortuitously including breeding pairs, it is implausible that they would have taken seedlings of plants that were already well established and abundant at the places they anticipated visiting. In fact, the presence of these plants in remote Polynesia shows that an accidental migration is beyond improbable, because the plants that were useful to the Polynesians did not occur naturally on any of the islands that were settled during the last period of Polynesian migration. This flora included not only the main food plants (yams, taro, bananas, and so on) but also trees that were crucial for textiles (such as pandanus and paper mulberry). Equally, other non-native plants—from turmeric (used both medicinally and as a dye), to candlenut (variously used as a dye for textiles, a tattoo pigment, and a source of oil), to kava (used to make a mildly narcotic drink)—were, and to varying degrees still are, all vital in Islanders' lives. There is no reason why those merely undertaking local voyages or going fishing would take the means of propagating this variety of species with them, but people intending to settle a new land had every reason to do so.

Andrew Sharp's critics also suggested that his book was tendentious: on the one hand exaggerating the hazards of ocean passages (the seasonality of severe storms is well understood) and impediments to navigation such as cloudy skies (in the Pacific most nights are typically clear); on the other, diminishing both the sailing capacity of historically documented vessels and Islanders' navigational abilities.[13]

In response, a remarkable mix of scholars, sailors, and Hawaiian cultural leaders took the debate out of the library and into a realm of truly heroic experimentation.[14] In 1973, the Polynesian Voyaging Society was founded in Hawai'i, and those involved undertook research and designed a double canoe based on a variety of historically documented Polynesian vessels. It was constructed of modern materials, yet in a manner intended to simulate the sailing capacities of a prehistoric oceangoing canoe as closely as possible. Contributing powerfully and evocatively to a broader cultural renaissance, the project sought to assess the capacity of such vessels to sail into the wind, which appeared essential given that the settlement of Polynesia followed a west-to-east path, into prevailing trade winds. The mariners also wanted to test customary navigational knowledge, which had lapsed over the many decades of colonization and depopulation throughout island Polynesia but was still alive in parts of Micronesia.

The vessel that would be called the *Hōkūle'a* sailed successfully on round-trip voyages from Hawaii to Tahiti in 1976 and 1980. The first journey was guided by Mau Piailug, an expert navigator from Satawal in the central Caroline Islands, who used standard modern instruments on the return leg. The second voyage was captained by Nainoa Thompson, a Hawaiian who had learned from Mau and reinvented a customary approach; on this trip, both the outward and return journeys were accomplished without instruments. Records gathered over the course of both voyages made it evident that Mau and Thompson were broadly accurate in their understandings of the *Hōkūle'a*'s location over the duration of the passages.

These ventures represented astonishing accomplishments and stimulated a wider range of canoe revivals and reenactments, such as the interisland voyages associated with the Festival of Pacific Arts. Voyaging has reemerged as a widely practiced expression of a living tradition. It is also a way for Islanders from diverse regions to share technical knowledge, ritual, and narrative and to express and extend deep cultural connections.

Yet what reenactments actually demonstrate in a robust scientific sense is less clear. With his *Kon-Tiki* expedition in 1947, Norwegian explorer Thor Heyerdahl proved that the type of raft used prehistorically and observed by the Spanish during the sixteenth century along the South American coast could reach the Tuamotu Archipelago. That does not mean that any similar vessel, or indeed any Indigenous American vessel at all, ever did so. (As was noted earlier, it is far more likely that the return voyage was undertaken by Islanders, from a Polynesian starting point.) The archaeologist Atholl Anderson has objected to a "traditionalism" that has come to frame much thinking about prehistoric seafaring. In his view, it is too easily assumed that the kinds of double canoes documented by Europeans in the eighteenth and nineteenth centuries existed centuries or millennia ago, that the vessels in use had the capacity to sail into the wind, and that exploratory return voyages were regularly undertaken.[15]

There are indeed enduring gaps in our understanding of how Lapita peoples reached Fiji and western Polynesia, and how their Polynesian successors subsequently colonized such distant islands as those of Hawai'i, Rapa Nui, and New Zealand. The documentation concerning the canoe types that were in use either in western Polynesia or in Hawai'i and Tahiti in the early decades of European contact provides us with only the most limited basis for speculating about what sorts of boats were used a thousand years earlier and, still less, three thousand years earlier. The apparent shifts in rig and sail structures in the Fiji-Tonga region in the late prehistoric and early European-contact periods suggest considerable innovation and dynamism, implying that technologies were unlikely to have stayed the same. If it is supposed that the sources of innovation lay outside the Pacific, in rigs and techniques developed by Indian Ocean or Southeast Asian traders and mariners, then these influences no doubt arrived and were adopted by Pacific Islanders only very gradually. But it is also quite possible—in the same way that people made the transition from foraging to agriculture independently in a number of different parts of the world—that heterogeneous approaches to the building of canoes and the manufacture of rigging developed at different times and in different places.

The *Hōkūle'a* voyages prove that some Polynesian canoes could sail effectively into the wind, but it is not certain that ancient seacraft had the capacity to do so. However, as Anderson notes, wind patterns have not been constant over time, and there have been periods when the El Niño southern oscillation created different conditions, including a reversal of the prevailing wind directions.[16] If it is difficult to make assumptions about what people knew or thought centuries or millennia ago, we can be confident that people who lived by, across, and on water understood the seas, currents, and winds intimately—just as farmers and pastoralists around the world today still have profound understandings of wind, weather, and seasonal change that city dwellers lack. If people were inclined to voyage, they would have been well aware of the range of seasonal conditions and of the variations they were subject to. They would have known when conditions were propitious for undertaking a particular voyage. They might have planned, but waited.

Scholars do Islanders no favors in wishfully evoking a falsely precise sense of how and why voyages were undertaken. It is certainly worth signaling a range of possibilities, which may or may not be susceptible to some form of rigorous testing. But much uncertainty is likely to endure. The environmental conditions across most of the Pacific simply do not favor the archaeological preservation of substantial timbers of any kind, let alone whole canoes of the sort used in interisland voyages. Although broken bits of canoes were occasionally used to mark graves, Oceanic ship burials like those of northern Europe—which resulted in relatively intact vessels being available for study—appear never to have been a feature of Pacific Island culture.

Although there is much that even further decades of archaeological work may never reveal, it is clear that the "accidental voyage" thesis can be dismissed. At the time Andrew Sharp's book was published, carbon dating was just beginning to clarify the sequence of island settlement. He cannot be faulted for not having taken into account the near-simultaneity of the first occupation of many islands in central-eastern Polynesia and the succeeding migrations into the extremities. Problematic as the drift-voyage argument remains on other grounds, it would be still harder to explain why, around 1000 AD, there would have been a spike in the number of accidental voyages that resulted in the settlement of many archipelagoes. Was one generation of seafarers singularly incompetent? To be sure, canoes certainly were lost, and survivors of shipwrecked voyages were sometimes cast away upon islands they never intended to visit. But such incidents do not model the settlement of the Pacific. That venture was one deliberately intended, conducted, and accomplished.

5

KNOWING THE OCEAN

THE NINETEENTH-CENTURY MISSIONARIES WHO SET OUT FROM Britain, determined to change peoples' beliefs, were, it is often assumed, narrow-minded and prejudiced characters. It is therefore something of a surprise and a relief to read one of the celebrities of the London Missionary Society, John Williams (1796–1839), on Islanders' navigational knowledge. The theme was of particular and practical importance to Williams, who had been born in London of an artisanal family but conceived the evangelical enterprise in the Pacific in highly ambitious terms. "The year 1821 was fraught with important events," Williams would write later. "It was, in fact, a year of great things." The people of Rurutu in the Austral Islands had renounced their ancestral beliefs and adopted Christianity seemingly spontaneously, without any involvement of missionaries, and there seemed scope as well for the conversion of the people of a whole archipelago, the Cook Islands. Williams had previously dropped two Society Islander missionaries, Papehia and Vahapatu, off on Aitutaki in the southern Cook Islands. He subsequently received letters from them calling for more workers and conveying news that there were people there who had come from another island, Rarotonga, and who had embraced the faith. This island—the largest of the Cook group—was yet to be visited by any European, and was known to the missionaries only through references in the "legendary tales" of the Society Islanders. Here, then, was at once an exploratory and an evangelical challenge.

Williams hired a vessel from merchants and recruited new Islander missionaries. At Aitutaki, it was learned that the Raiatean teachers had already obtained dramatic results: ancestral temples had been destroyed, images of deities burned or surrendered to the missionaries, and a chapel some two hundred feet in length already erected. Williams and his group proceeded in search of Rarotonga, which they failed to locate, but called at Mangaia and the smaller islands of Mitiaro, Mauke, and Atiu, where they left Polynesian teachers to carry on the work. At Atiu, a high chief named Rongomatane volunteered to direct them to Rarotonga, which he said was just a day-and-a-half's sail away. Williams was initially perplexed by the chief's responses to inquiries as to the island's location, as he seemed at different times to point in quite different directions.

But this was soon explained; for the natives, in making their voyages, do not leave from any part of an island, as we do, but, invariably, have what may be called starting-points. At these places they have certain land-marks, by which they steer, until the stars become visible; and they generally contrive to set sail so as to get sight of their heavenly guides by the time their land-marks disappear. Knowing this, we determined to adopt the native plan, and steered our vessel round to the 'starting-point'. Having arrived there, the chief was desired to look to the land-marks, while the vessel was being turned gradually round; and when his marks on the shore ranged with each other, he cried out, 'That's it! that is it.' I looked immediately at the compass, and found the course to be S.W. by W.; and it proved to be as correct as if he had been an accomplished navigator.[1]

By which Williams presumably meant, an accomplished navigator in the European sense. He added that the case demonstrated "the correctness of native knowledge," but that it was essential that the people were "allowed to communicate it in their own particular way." This, too, was insightful: although Islanders had shared their knowledge of geography and other matters with early visitors to a remarkable extent, there was far more that might have been documented, had the style of interaction been less hierarchical, had questions more often been asked in a less interrogative way, and had Europeans been more open to what perhaps seemed like irrational, inconsistent, or roundabout ways of responding.

Williams was nevertheless not alone: many explorers, missionaries, and ethnologists were fundamentally impressed by Islanders' ability to identify direction and by their knowledge of the stars. But others were disparaging, and over the nineteenth century, European travelers' and ethnologists' commentary around these themes tended to be contradictory. Just as there was often a fundamental assumption that ancient Islanders' boats could not have been good enough—despite the testimonials of Dampier and Cook—to undertake long, open-ocean voyages, so it was also presumed that Indigenous navigation could not have been sufficiently sophisticated to guide canoes successfully beyond the range of relatively shorter voyages.

Though that view was tainted by its denigration of Islanders' achievements, it could not be directly refuted because Polynesian navigational knowledge had never been precisely documented. Especially in eastern Polynesia, local populations had suffered catastrophic depopulation, caused by introduced diseases that had a severe impact across many islands and archipelagoes from the late eighteenth century onward. On Rapa Nui, the impact was compounded by the kidnapping of Islanders, who were enslaved in Peru. The collapse of Pacific Island populations meant that cultural knowledge, including specialist priestly and navigational knowledge, was lost—as were particular arts, such as those of canoe construction. In any case, the building of larger canoes tended to lapse as European ships were increasingly used for longer journeys—although smaller fishing canoes continued to be made, and are still made today, in many parts of the Pacific.

When the anthropologist Ben Finney and others sought to reenact ancient voyages, they turned to Micronesia, and the Caroline Islands in particular, following the lead of the New Zealand doctor and sailor David Lewis, the first outsider to recognize, in the 1960s, the importance of the navigational knowledge that some Pacific Islanders preserved.[2]

On the basis of extended voyages with local navigators Tevake and Hipour, Lewis codified the core issues and principles of distant navigation without instruments. While successful navigators were bearers of formidable astronomical and maritime knowledge, their competence could be distilled into three key areas: they had to master the arts, first, of orientation or course setting; second, of maintaining a course once identified; and third, of making landfall.[3]

John Williams's anecdote regarding the guidance of the chief Rongomatane underscores the importance of local knowledge of place—including bearings on land—to the basic challenge of orientation. This may be counterintuitive for a non-Indigenous person who is used to maps. As Williams implied, Europeans were accustomed to using cartographic representations to locate themselves wherever they happened to be; thus, starting points were arbitrary. In contrast, Rongomatane could, from a specific departure point, evidently visually triangulate the correct orientation. Often hills or other natural landmarks enabled navigators to set direction, but large stones are also known to have been placed and aligned so as to facilitate orientation—this is, for example, documented on the atoll of Arorae in southern Kiribati, which lacks elevated landmarks.[4]

The stars were also fundamental to precise course setting. They rise in the east and set in the west, and, unlike the rising and setting positions of the sun and moon, those points and trajectories are essentially unvarying. The navigator thus needed to know which star had the same bearing as the target island. As that star rose, it would provide a directional fix; the navigator would need to understand which

Men on the outrigger platform of a Marshall Islands canoe, 1900.

other stars provided appropriate points of reference when the original star rose too high, was out of view as a result of cloud cover, or had dropped below the horizon. If a canoe was being pushed off course by currents or winds, the navigator had to have a sense of how far these forces would shift the vessel. In our terms, if we were being pushed off course by five degrees to port, directing the canoe toward a destination star five degrees off the starboard side from one aligned with the true destination would compensate, keeping the vessel on course. But the corrective steer would, needless to say, require a finely tuned capacity to sense the effects of the forces acting on the vessel. Even an inexperienced sailor can tell whether or not a boat is on course when it is within sight of land—that is, with a fixed point of reference in view. But the capacity to make such judgements in the absence of visible markers reflects a truly impressive sensitivity to the marine environment. The Arorae stones were aligned off the true directions to their target islands, apparently in order to compensate for dominant currents.

Assuming that conditions were not dead calm, mariners would also pay close attention to the predominant wave pattern as their voyage progressed. Winds would often generate cross-cutting disturbance—that is, a choppy sea—but

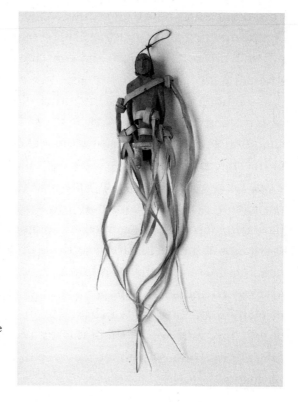

Hos, navigator's weather charm, late nineteenth or early twentieth century, Lamotrek atoll, Yap archipelago, Caroline Islands.

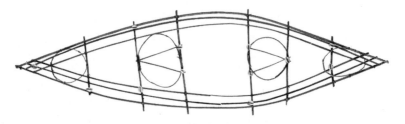

Navigation chart, Ailinglaplap atoll, Marshall Islands, nineteenth century.

experienced sailors could readily discern the underlying swell. The latter was typically constant over great reaches of open ocean and would thus provide a vital point of reference, complementing other indicators that a navigator would note not only through deliberate and conscious observation, but through native physical awareness. Just as someone "feels" the weather around them (a mounting wind, a sudden chill, mist turning to rain), so a navigator could sense the natural conditions, particularly those that made a critical difference to the success or failure of the voyage. Such were the intuitions born of a life spent on water, dedicated to the art of navigation. A canoe's course and progress would certainly have been formally determined and monitored, through observations of the sky as careful as those undertaken by European mariners with their instruments, but that passage was also sensed and felt. Of course, mariners everywhere, especially those piloting smaller ships, are attuned to conditions at sea, but awareness of them was always more fundamentally critical to those without recourse to instrument-based navigation.

Based on what he understood of customary Caroline Islands traditions, David Lewis argued that Islanders followed something like the method of dead reckoning employed by European mariners before longitude could be accurately determined. Once a course was set, typically along a line of latitude, a log (in a literal sense—a block of wood at the end of a rope) was employed to estimate speed, and the position of the ship was plotted daily. The Caroline Islands system measured progress not on the basis of velocity but conceptually, in relation to a reference island that was neither the departure point nor the destination. This island would be at some bearing from the canoe, such as northeast in western terms, which would become east and then southeast as the passage progressed. The traveling canoe successively reached different bearings in relation to the reference island; at each point, the island would be underneath a specific setting star, although it could not actually be seen. Finney cites the instance of a passage of some 120 miles between Woleai and Olimarao atolls in Micronesia. The island of Faraulep is virtually equidistant from both and serves as the reference island for the relatively short voyage, but it was in fact well out of sight from the beginning to the end of the journey. The island was, in effect, an abstract point, but one that enabled the navigator to visualize movement through a number of stages (*etak*), six in the case of that passage.[5] A walker may have a mental map of a landscape he or she traverses; this was a sort of mental chart, but one consisting of a moving relationship between named places, not by a track across a space.

Such records of traditional way-finding methods imply a truly formidable practical understanding of heavenly bodies and their movements, and an intimate sense of air and water, particularly of the varying and shifting strength of winds and currents. The combination of calculation and sensory familiarity with the environment was critical to one of the most basic questions of any voyage: How close is the destination?

Once the navigator had a sense that a canoe was approaching an island target, he—and no doubt others on board—would keenly observe the water and the sky for signs of any landmass. The pattern of waves might vary, stacks of cloud could suggest land, and larger and higher islands would alter the winds. The summits of Orohena and Mauna Kea, the highest mountains on Tahiti and the Big Island of Hawai'i, reach 7,352 and 13,802 feet, respectively. The islands and their associated cloud formations are thus readily visible from considerable distances. If the destination is an atoll, with land barely meters above sea level and palms only a little higher, birds provide indications of land long before the island itself comes into view.

Islanders were fortunate that the geological forces at work beneath the Pacific tended to produce archipelagoes such as those of Samoa, Tonga, the Marquesas, and Hawai'i. Islands thus mostly came in groups, although there are some islands that stand on their own, including Rapa Nui. An archipelago constituted a broad target; once a canoe reached any part of it, the course could be adjusted toward the particular island and landing point sought. The relative density of the Tuamotuan atolls must, to some extent, have alleviated the risk of missing any one destination island.

Knowledge and methods of these kinds would also have enabled exploratory voyages in search of new islands: a canoe could travel into unknown seas as far as was considered practical and then be able to find the way home. Whether this strategy was adopted, or whether prospective settlers simply gambled on reaching land before their water and food were exhausted, we cannot know. But the sweet potato would certainly not have been cultivated in eastern Polynesia had some return voyages to coastal South America not taken place, implying that such expeditions were at least episodically attempted.

In 1778, Johann Reinhold Forster published a version of a chart drawn by Tupaia, the Society Islander who had interacted extensively with Cook, Banks, Banks's artists, and other members of the *Endeavour* crew while the ship was based at Tahiti from April to July 1769, before joining the expedition on its onward passage to New Zealand and beyond. Forster was a complicated character, but he was unstinting in his celebration of Polynesian civilization and in particular of this graphic expression of Indigenous knowledge. He offered the engraving of the map to the public as "a monument of the ingenuity and geographical knowledge" of the Islanders.[6] This published version and, more particularly, a manuscript copy attributed to James Cook of an "original" chart prepared by Tupaia himself, together with associated lists of islands and other records, have been at the very center of scholarly inquiry into, and argument about, Pacific geographical knowledge ever since. Especially over the last seventy years or so, archaeologists, historians, art historians,

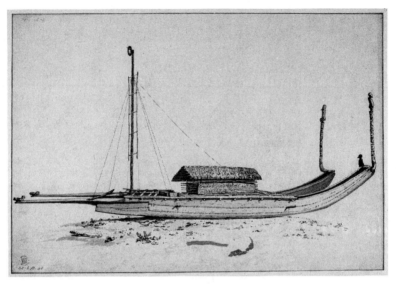

Tahitian canoe drawn by John Webber, during Cook's third voyage.

ethnographers, sailing enthusiasts, and (most recently) postcolonial, literary, and Indigenous scholars have weighed in on the debate.[7]

At one level, the diagram is simple enough: it provides an indication of islands known to Tupaia. Although some of the mariners were not bad linguists, basic problems arise from their varying ability to recognize local phonetics and the lack of a standardized approach to spelling Pacific names and words in the period. Some island names are readily recognizable and some can be reasonably inferred; others, however, remain obscure. According to Cook, Tupaia knew of some 130 islands. Seventy-four appear on Cook's transcription of the map, although some may be depicted twice. Those that are straightforwardly identifiable include the other islands of the Society group; Rangiroa, Hao, and Fakarava in the Tuamotu Islands; Tubuai and Rurutu in the Austral Islands; Manihiki and Rarotonga in the Cook Islands; and Fatu Hiva, Hiva Oa, and Nuku Hiva in the Marquesas. It is striking that comparatively detailed knowledge extended as far as the major archipelagoes of western Polynesia. Vavaʻu and all the major Samoan Islands are listed. But in fact, nothing is simple about this sheet of paper. To start with, it is less a single map than part of an archive of surviving and lost documents, including draft maps, copies, and various lists of islands—the legacies of a remarkable, but incompletely recorded, series of inquiries, conversations, and cartographic collaborations involving not only Tupaia and Cook but others aboard the *Endeavour*. These dialogues

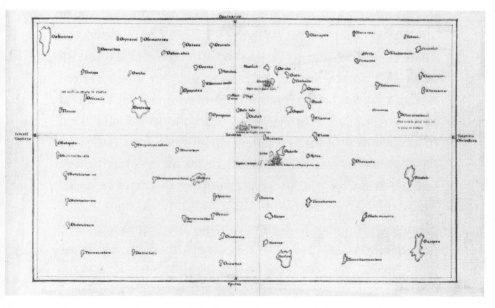

Tupaia's map; this copy, made by Captain James Cook, is in the British Library.

were enlarged over time: the islands known to particular Islanders were asked after and transcribed on Cook's second and third voyages, but also contemporaneously by the Spanish and subsequently by a variety of other more or less inquisitive voyagers.

The lists and charts raise the question, first, of in what sense the places named were "known." Some—such as within the Society Islands archipelago itself and the Tuamotus to the northeast—were visited more or less frequently. They were part of the wider networks that constituted Tahitian social, ritual, and exchange systems. It appears that at least the nearer parts of the Austral Islands were similarly connected. When John Webber, the Royal Academician on Cook's third voyage, depicted the ceremony of human sacrifice that Cook witnessed on September 1, 1777, his illustration included standing drums that are undoubtedly of an Austral Islands type. Whether these were made in the Australs (most likely on Ra'ivavae) and brought to Tahiti, or made in Tahiti by Austral Islander craftsmen who had traveled or relocated to Tahiti, they indicate some sort of contact between the two island groups. Had the watercolor been made twenty years later, this evidence would have been ambiguous, as the drum bringers or drum makers might have taken advantage of European shipping to travel between the islands. From the mid to late 1790s onward, merchants' passages through the region became more frequent, and Islanders took advantage of the opportunities to join those ships and travel within and beyond the Pacific. But at the time the ceremony was witnessed, there were no passages between the islands, other than on Islanders' canoes.

There is thus strong evidence, in addition to the charts and the island lists, for continuing interactions among these archipelagoes. This is less clear, however, with respect to many other islands that are named in eighteenth-century records. Across the Pacific, and particularly in Polynesia, narratives of migration and origin were socially significant. They documented and affirmed distinctions of rank, connections among descendants, and rights to particular resources and sites. Such traditions were commonly replete with place names and island names. Some customary historians may have had an awareness of these islands' locations, and perhaps those with more specialized navigational knowledge were aware of the starting points, orientations, and stars that would enable a sailor to reach their harbors. Whether these islands were regularly visited, or had been visited any time recently, is another matter. In other words, the charts and lists identified places that were known in different ways: some on the basis of actual visits; others as places known to have been visited, but perhaps not by the people who provided the information; and still others that were recorded traditionally, alive in people's imagined geographies though essentially beyond the realm of actual travel. This last group included real places, yet people knew about them through the oral equivalent of literary citation. In the same way, educated Europeans of the medieval or early modern periods knew of places in Asia Minor through the *Odyssey* and Herodotus's *Histories*, or through literary works that drew on those sources, but had little sense of how such places would be reached and no notion that they themselves might attempt to do so.

What is recorded regarding Tupaia's own travels reinforces this picture, and indeed its ambiguity. The sources
are clear that he had visited, and presumably traveled extensively among, all the major islands in the Societies group:
Moorea (which neighbors Tahiti), Bora Bora, Tahaa, Huahine, Ra'iatea (from which he himself originated), Maupiti
(the most distant island to the west), Mehetia (a smaller
island to the east), and Teti'aroa (the atoll to the north, famously a place of resort for Tahitian aristocrats).[8] Tupaia
had also been to Rurutu—and piloted the *Endeavour*
there—and was said also to have been to Tubuai, but he did
not know islands farther south, such as Rapa.[9]

An oblique reference in Cook's journal also suggests
that Tupaia had voyaged as far as Tonga. He told Cook that
if they sailed from Ra'iatea toward the west they should

> meet with plenty of Islands, the most of them he has
> himself been at and from the description he gives of
> two of them they must be those discover'd by Captain
> Wallice [Wallis] and by him call'd Boscawen and Kepple
> Islands, and these do not lay less than 400 Leagues to
> the westward of Ulietea [Ra'iatea]; he says that they
> are 10 or 12 days in going thither and 30 or more in
> coming back and that their Paheas [*pahi*], that is their
> large Proas sails much faster than this Ship; all this I
> believe to be true and therefore they may with ease sail
> 40 Leagues a day or more.[10]

Wallis's islands are Tafahi and Niuatoputapu, at the
northern extremity of the Tongan archipelago. Tupaia's

"description" presumably referred to a pair of neighboring high islands; he may have made it clear that the smaller of the two was in the form of a classic, conical volcano. If Cook was correct regarding the speed of larger Tahitian voyaging canoes, they would have sailed some 140 miles a day, and indeed been able to journey from Ra'iatea to Niuatoputapu in ten to twelve days—the distance is 1,479 miles, scarcely more than Cook's broad estimate of four hundred leagues. The figures thus support the view that Tupaia and others had voyaged from the Societies as far as these islands, and perhaps elsewhere in western Polynesia. Yet there is little in the way of complementary evidence for such voyages, and little to indicate that there were regular contacts, or, at the time of Cook's visits, any recent contacts between the Society Islands and the Marquesas (slightly over two-thirds the distance from the Society group to Tonga) or the Cook Islands (around half the distance).

Although Tupaia's chart raises questions of many kinds, it is also enigmatic in the most basic sense, in that the principles of its visual organization are not what they seem. Since the eighteenth century, European visitors have looked at it as though it were a European map—an image of situated landmasses from above that are objectively distributed rather than seen from a single perspective. Tupaia's chart was not that kind of map. The places on it are distributed according to a distinct logic that is difficult to discern, not least because the extant versions of the chart were evidently manipulated, but not in ways that can be specifically recognized and undone.

A recent study appears to make a breakthrough in clarifying the layout of the diagram. Lars Eckstein and Anja

Schwarz have argued that, while Tupaia was starting from a chart laid out in European terms, with north at the top, this was not the visual order within which he wished to accommodate his sense of the ocean.[11] They do not propose that his map exemplifies Polynesian cartography, but suggest rather that Tupaia—who by this time was well aware of European mapmaking and its methods of daily calculation, which notably involved a somewhat ritualistic, public set of observations at exactly noon—came up with an "ingenious" and innovative system, at once true to the situated knowledge he articulated and intelligible to the European mariners he had come to know. The vital clue, for Eckstein and Schwarz, is the presence of an apparent island labeled "Avatea" right in the center of the composition. But *avatea* was not an island; the word refers to noon, and Johann Forster had in fact recorded that it was "the line where the sun comes closest to their zenith." Although not the most crucial marker for Polynesian navigators, noon observations were important, as they enabled confirmation of a canoe's bearing. The islands across the chart are thus situated in relation to *avatea*.

Eckstein and Schwarz also argue that lists of island names enable a larger decoding of the chart. The order of islands in the various manuscript records of conversations is not arbitrary, they suggest, but reflects a series of staging points on longer voyages. As they put it, "Sequence is paramount."[12] Based on these predicates, they pick out sections of the chart that they consider to represent voyages to various parts of the Cook Islands, the Australs, Samoa, and

Hawai'i. Seeking corroboration from mythic and traditional sources, they aim to offer a sort of evidentiary triangulation among these texts, island lists, and routes hidden within the "island cloud" of Tupaia's chart. The argument is rich in inference regarding the interpretation of names, Tupaia's intentions as he prepared various versions of the chart, and the conversations he may have been having with the Europeans at the time. Eckstein and Schwarz's project is imaginative and engaging, but it must be seen as a thought experiment. As commentators have remarked, every step on their discursive journey moves from conjecture to speculation. It is a journey that is markedly reminiscent of Abraham Fornander's: formidable in its extent, yet constructed out of identifications, links, and affinities that are now and then plausible but more often appear contrived.

The argument evokes eighteenth-century Tahiti as a hub for voyages that connected vast swaths of Polynesia, including not only the more proximate archipelagoes of the Tuamotus and the Australs, but also Hawai'i, the Marquesas, and western Polynesia. This is, many would argue, a case of over-inference, but other problems arise. The rich and extensive archives—the records of travelers, missionaries, and ethnologists, together with local oral histories—that document society, culture, and history across these island groups tell us much about exchange networks, extra-local contacts, and canoe voyages. This body of evidence clearly documents certain voyaging routes, but it does not support regular, long-distance voyaging—for instance, between Tahiti and Hawai'i.

These archives—which incorporate a range of Indigenous sources as well as outsiders' observations—are fragmented, dispersed, and not always easy to interpret. However, those seeking to understand, for example, Marquesan life in the period prior to colonial invasion and disruption are fortunate to have the extensive and nuanced accounts of the missionary William Pascoe Crook, who spent some eighteen months in the islands, from mid-1797 to early 1799, and of the beachcomber Edward Robarts, who lived there for over seven years, from 1798 to 1806. Both spent time in both the southern and northern sections of the archipelago, and their records are complementary. Crook was a gentleman scholar who drew on interviews with a young Marquesan, Teimoteitei, who accompanied him back to England. Crook's account incorporates an overview of Marquesan "manners and customs," whereas Robarts's text, although not strictly a journal, provides a fine-grain account of day-to-day circumstances and relationships among the Islanders, whom he came to know intimately.

Some years later, David Porter—the American naval officer who mounted an extraordinary attack against the Taipi of Nuku Hiva in 1813 and claimed the island for the United States—thought that Marquesans knew the names of only six islands beyond the group. Whether that is correct or not, both Crook and Robarts evoke an Indigenous world that featured high levels of interaction within both the northern and southern clusters of the group. Certainly, the people of the southern islands of Tahuata and Hiva Oa exchanged visits very frequently and were connected through bonds between allied groups and through long-standing feuds with enemies on the neighboring islands. It is also clear from Robarts's narrative that there were occasional voyages from Nuku Hiva to Tahuata—in part to barter "loaves" of prepared turmeric for other products. Given that this passage took only a couple of days, such voyages seem to have been surprisingly infrequent. But neither of these accounts alludes to inter-archipelagic voyaging.

According to Robarts, however, some people responded to periods of famine or great social stress by emigrating. His narrative of his return journey to Nuku Hiva following a visit to 'Ua Pou describes a canoe heavily laden with valuables of some sort. The sailors' intention was to purchase larger canoes, "for the purpose," as he put it in an account both skeptical and sentimental, "of leaveing their country to go in scearch of other land, where plenty of food is abounding. The prophet pretends to have seen in a dream fine countrys a few days sailing distant. This the poor deluded people believe and leave in numbers the lands that gave them breath."[13]

This makes it clear that people might undertake distant voyages of relocation and new settlement, venturing beyond the islands known to them. But it appears—at this period of Polynesian history—that they did so out of duress, rather than other aims such as social interaction. Unless Robarts has misinterpreted or misrepresented the knowledge of the "prophet" (the *tau'a*, or shaman), his account also implies that the people of the Marquesas did not have specific knowledge of islands and archipelagoes beyond their own island group.

Similarly, the important testimony of the *Bounty* mutineer James Morrison—who resided in the Society Islands for just under two years—points to both the reach and the limitations of Society Islander voyages the early 1790s. He described the impressive canoes and the trading expeditions they undertook to the Tuamotus to obtain pearl shell, among other goods, noting that "some of the Islands they sail to are at the Distance of more than 100 leagues." He elaborated:

> The Chief of *Taiarapu* [a Tahitian district] keeps one of these vessels constantly plying between *Tahiti* and *Me'etia*, Calld by us Osnaburgh Island, 27 leages SE of Taheite, which is Subject to Him. . . . They have Communication with several others to the NE of Tahiti and taking the advantage of the Northerly Wind reach *Me'etia* where they watch the Wind shifting to stretch to the Northward to a Group of small Islands, the Capital of which is Calld *Tapuhoe*.[14]

This is drawn from a more extensive passage that also refers to regular traffic with the atoll of Teti'aroa. Morrison, like Cook and other writers of the period, was unstinting in acknowledging Polynesian navigational expertise, in terms that many others subsequently reiterated: the Polynesians' capacity to predict weather reflected "amazing sagacity," and they were able to shape a course "with some degree of exactness." This makes what Morrison says and does not say all the more significant. If people *did* sail to islands that were more than "100 leagues" away, the implication is that they *did not* sail to islands that were substantially more distant. One hundred nautical leagues is 345 miles. The implied range would embrace the Tuamotus and Rurutu, but not the Marquesas, which are almost three times as far away.

The range of Polynesian voyaging in the late eighteenth century is similarly reflected by an incident during Cook's third voyage, on which Cook was charged with bringing home a young man of Ra'iatea named Mai (Omai), following his celebrated visit to England. In April 1777, the ship called briefly at Atiu, a small island northeast of Rarotonga in the Cook Islands. There, Mai

> met with four of his country men . . . who about ten years ago were coming from Otaheite to Ulietea [Ra'iatea] but missing the latter, were after being at sea a long time, cast ashore upon this. There were twenty in the whole men and women in the Canoes, but only five survived. . . . Providence brought them in sight of the people of this island, who sent out Canoes to bring them a shore, where they were kindly treated, and were now so well satisfied with their situation that they refused the offer which Omai made of giving them a passage with us to their native isle.[15]

All evidence of this kind is open to interpretation, but the circumstances hardly imply that regular voyages linked Atiu or others of the Cook Islands with Tahiti in this period. Indeed, the broader range of historic evidence reinforces a long-standing archaeological argument, albeit one forgotten in the most recent exegeses of Tupaia's map. This argument contends that, post-settlement, two-way voyaging may have been initially extensive, maintaining contacts between widely separated archipelagoes, but that it was largely abandoned by the eighteenth century. This observation in no way diminishes the incredible achievements of either the first Islander voyagers, who sailed across vast expanses of open ocean, or their successors, who came to know inhabited seas intimately. It is, rather, understandable that as the populations of island groups such as the Societies and the Marquesas grew, greater density enabled the peoples of neighboring islands to generate new realms of exchange and periodic social and ceremonial interaction. Relationships with those in more distant communities of origin became less significant.

The decades of ongoing controversy around the seagoing capacities of canoes, the precise extent of Polynesian geographic knowledge, and the meanings and implications of Tupaia's chart reflect intense interest in Islanders' voyages. Today, that interest is shared by scholars and academics, by those engaged in reenacting voyages, and by Pacific communities who are inspired by these expressions of history, identity, and knowledge. The debates matter, and they are likely to be sustained. The sheer complexity of the evidence and the underlying issues of cross-cultural research methodologies mean that none of the larger questions are likely to be resolved anytime soon. But contentious debate has also obscured the extent to which a consensus has been reached on some key issues.

First, claims regarding American origins or significant American influence in the Pacific can be laid to rest. The presence of sweet potato in eastern Polynesia makes it clear

Marovo Lagoon, Solomon Islands, 1998.

that there were some prehistoric contacts between the peoples of South America and Islanders. Yet, given the voyaging propensities of both peoples, it is now recognized that it is far more likely that Islanders undertook perhaps just one, or a few, voyages to American coasts, bringing this important plant back with them and no doubt interacting in other ways with the people of the continent.

Second, there is no doubt that accidental voyages took place and may have been comparatively common, but they were not the means by which the islands of the Pacific were settled. From its Ice Age beginnings, the human colonization of the Pacific was deliberately conceived and undertaken. What motivated those who embarked on these voyages constitutes one of the major enigmas of human history. For the Lapita people and their descendants, the principle that the founders of communities gained great mana and secured high status for those of their line goes some way toward explaining why people might take the risk of venturing into unknown tracts of ocean in search of new homes. But it does not help us understand why, at specific times, the Lapita colonists and later the Polynesians' ancestors should launch—from the Bismarck Islands and western Polynesia, respectively—waves of colonizing voyages that took Islanders unprecedented distances to a host of new islands and archipelagoes. Advances in dating have made it clear that, in the *longue durée* of human history, these people expanded their range almost suddenly, establishing new communities across a wide range of previously unvisited islands within a few generations. What prompted these energetic, outward moves appears obscure now and may remain so.

In the early 1990s, Epeli Hau'ofa rejected pessimistic views of the Pacific Islands in disciplines such as development studies and economics. Academics in these fields viewed Oceania as isolated, unsustainable, too small, and too far away. But Hau'ofa evoked the inspiring reality, over centuries, of lives lived across Oceania. Now scholarship in history, anthropology, and archaeology is fully supportive of his vision. As he wrote of Islanders:

Theirs was a large world in which peoples and cultures moved and mingled, unhindered by boundaries of the kind erected much later by imperial powers. From one island to another they sailed to trade and to marry, thereby expanding social networks for greater flows of wealth. They travelled to visit relatives in a wide variety of natural and cultural surroundings, to quench their thirst for adventure, and even to fight and dominate. . . .

This was the kind of world that bred men and women with skills and courage that took them into the unknown, to discover and populate all the habitable islands east of the 130th meridian. The great fame that they have earned posthumously may have been romanticized, but it is solidly based on real feats that could have been performed only by those born and raised with an open sea as their home.[16]

EPILOGUE

On Tupaia Street

IN DECEMBER 2016, ABOUT A WEEK BEFORE CHRISTMAS, I WAS with a group of Aboriginal representatives from the La Perouse community, in southern Sydney. We sat drinking coffee under a big awning at a pavement café opposite a grand pub, the Sir Joseph Banks Hotel. We were not far from the shores of Botany Bay, the site of the first encounter between the Indigenous Australians of the east coast and the participants in Captain Cook's voyages in April 1770. The suburb was itself called Botany, commemorating Banks's science. We were talking about those first contacts, which were confrontational. Two Gweagal warriors had thrown spears, resisting Cook's landing, but on being shot at they withdrew. Our discussion focused on a debate concerning a set of spears that members of Cook's party had then appropriated. But that is another story. I mention the occasion here only because, once our meeting had finished, I walked down the street with a colleague from

Canberra who had offered me a lift back into the city center. Her car was parked in a broad side street dominated by mature eucalyptus trees shading mostly modest bungalows that probably dated from the 1940s. It seemed wonderfully appropriate that this was Tupia [*sic*] Street. In Canada, New Zealand, and Australia, Cook memorials and streets named after the navigator and various crew members are abundant. This was the first time I had encountered any commemoration of the *Endeavour*'s Polynesian fellow traveler. The street name perhaps reflected interest on the local city council at the time of the 1970s bicentennial.

We could consider Tupaia Street to be not only an out-of-the-way location in Sydney's southeast, but a metaphorical space. In the 1950s, Andrew Sharp's book provoked intense debate regarding Islanders' navigational knowledge, maritime skills, canoe technologies, and settlement histories. Interest in those themes already had a long history, and their exploration was subsequently sustained by a mix of practicing sailors (from David Lewis to those who took the *Hōkūle'a* across the Pacific), scientists, and Indigenous advocates of cultural renaissance. Over the last thirty years, a new movement across history, anthropology, archaeology, and Pacific studies has highlighted the entangled nature of exploration and encounter in Oceania over recent centuries. In this context, Tupaia has become a foundational figure. Though much of his biography remains obscure to us, he was certainly a remarkable, creative, and innovative individual, keenly interested in sharing knowledge and, in particular, communicating Polynesian geographic understanding to peoples who had only recently appeared from beyond his known world. Alongside his engaging illustrations of places, scenes, and people, his manifestly extraordinary yet enduringly enigmatic chart has become an icon of the moment. Those of us intrigued by cross-cultural encounters, Oceania's deep histories, and the reactivation of culture and knowledge could all be said to be on Tupaia Street, making sense of his legacy, and the legacies of many other voyagers, in sometimes unexpected places.

This book has offered a brief survey of a particular chapter of humanity's history: the settlement of the islands of the Pacific. A different approach could have been limited to what is now known with certainty. I have aimed to introduce what is known, but also to reflect on what has been at stake in inquiries of this kind over the last few hundred years. One point that is obvious should nevertheless be made: research continues. Methods in archaeology and related fields become ever more sophisticated. Fieldwork, increasingly undertaken through close partnerships with local institutions and communities in Pacific nations and territories, will continue to refine, and perhaps overturn, current understandings. Even so, *Voyagers* points toward three broad conclusions.

First, investigation into these areas was a cross-cultural business from its very beginnings. Not only Tupaia but a considerable number of other Islanders provided lists of island names and discussed voyaging with inquisitive foreign visitors. Such dialogues were to be sustained. For all his faults, Abraham Fornander celebrated the knowledge of the Hawaiians he worked with and learned extensively from them. Te Rangihiroa was a Maori scholar, and he combined what he had learned from fieldwork with Islanders in many parts of Polynesia together with the concepts and methods of early twentieth-century museum ethnology. The Polynesian Voyaging Society engaged Micronesian customary expertise in what was essentially a Hawaiian project; the summative book on the society's achievements up to the early 1990s was written primarily by Ben Finney, who acknowledged eleven mainly Indigenous coauthors. In 2020, the "decolonization" of anthropology and other social science and humanities disciplines is a focus of campus campaigning. Academics have been challenged to recognize Indigenous knowledge and to work toward what is referred to as the "coproduction" of new understanding. The history of ideas regarding identity, migration, ethnicity, and race in Oceania can be described only as messy and can certainly be troubling at times. Yet this history demonstrates that the coproduction of knowledge is not new. We should not be surprised that Indigenous knowledge has been central to our understanding of Oceania for so long.

Islander populations were typically small in global terms. Yet the Pacific is vast: the ocean and its archipelagoes occupy a third of the world's surface. The second conclusion that might be drawn from the story of the region is that, in the deepest possible sense, human histories exhibit many strands and trajectories; they exemplify diversity. Many people are skeptical about notions of progress, but the sense that humanity has made a series of singular, decisive advances—from tool use, through the invention of agriculture, to the emergence of civilization in the first cities, to the development of manufacturing industry and

A Maori woman welcomes the *Hokul'ea* and *Hikianalia*, two Hawaiian voyaging canoes, at Waitangi in the North Island of New Zealand, November 2014.

the globalization of economies—has remained tenacious. Those advances saw a baton passed from Africa to southwest Asia to the Mediterranean and then to Europe. In the 1970s, the discovery of early agriculture in the New Guinea Highlands was—together with analogous findings in other parts of the world—decisively important in empowering a genuinely plural sense of humanity's economic, social, and cultural innovation. The sheer singularity of Oceania's ways of life—based in, on, and across water—underscores this vision further. Islanders' maritime achievements were judged by those who were well equipped to do so, such as William Dampier, as astonishing. Despite lacking metal tools, they were the makers of the "best of any boats in the world." Oceania was not only a distinctive civilization, but an inhabited realm that speaks the plurality and diversity of human culture.

Third, the deep and more recent histories of the Pacific are powerfully suggestive, with respect to questions of identity. In 1624, John Donne famously wrote

No man is an island,
Entire of itself.
Every man is a piece of the continent,
A part of the main.

This sense that an island is cut off by definition, profoundly separate from other lands and human realms, has arguably been fundamental to the imagining of islands in the West for centuries, if not longer—witness Daniel Defoe's *Robinson Crusoe*, in which individuality is exemplified by the eponymous character's insular isolation. But the whole history of the Pacific tells us something very different about being an Islander. Those we call Islanders could in fact nearly all be better described as inter-Islanders or archipelago dwellers. Pacific peoples formed communities with neighbors from nearby or more distant islands that were almost without exception linked through kinship, ceremony, and exchange networks, as well as through relations of contest and hostility. An exception is the people of Rapa Nui, who were

Fidel Yoringmal and his grandson, Walla Island. Malekula, Vanuatu, 2011.

not in regular contact with others, but their situation was virtually unique. While the range and reach of voyaging over recent centuries is unclear, and may be exaggerated in some evocations, it is nevertheless the case that across the Pacific people interacted extensively within and between archipelagoes. While their voyages often involved trade, Islanders' traffic was—as Bronisław Malinowski famously recognized in the Trobriand Islands of New Guinea—socially motivated.

People undertook voyages to initiate, sustain, and extend relationships. Those relationships were the principal form of achievement within the societies concerned, bringing successful voyagers fame and renown.

The settlement of the Pacific over thousands of years certainly represents an incredible series of accomplishments. From another perspective, the most profound and important achievement of Oceanic civilization was not voyaging but this social principle: that what matters most in life is not separate identity, but our capacity to connect.

ACKNOWLEDGMENTS

Nearly forty years ago, as a student in Canberra, I became fascinated by the Pacific and by the achievements of Pacific Islanders, past and present. I cannot possibly thank the many teachers, colleagues, friends, hosts, and research partners, in the Pacific and elsewhere, who have supported my interests since. I was first inspired by Jack Golson, preeminent among archaeologists of the Pacific of his generation and a friend of my parents. Warmest thanks also to Peter Bellwood, who introduced me to Pacific archaeology as an undergraduate, Patrick Kirch, whose rich and textured studies have long been inspiring, and Pierre and Marie-Noëlle Ottino, who helped me make a home (and a base for my doctoral research) on the island of 'Ua Pou in the Marquesas in the early 1980s. Early on, Pat, Pierre, and Marie-Noëlle moreover gave me tours of archaeological projects in progress in Hawai'i and the Marquesas. This sense of the intimate context of the Polynesian past in environments still today shaped by Islanders' values and lives has remained with me ever since. I am indebted above all to Matthew Spriggs for his friendship and for conversations over many years about Pacific archaeology, history, politics, and much else.

I was honored to know Ben Finney (1933–2017) and Herb Kāne (1928–2011), founding members of the Polynesian Voyaging Society; conversations with them were inspiring. Most recently, I am immensely grateful to Peter Brunt, Noelle Kahanu, Emmanuel Kasarhérou, Sean Mallon, Michael Mel, and Anne Salmond for contributions to the 2018 "Oceania" exhibition that I co-curated with Peter, which shaped the understanding of the region that informs this book. I am deeply indebted to Helen Alderson and Dylan Gaffney, practicing archaeologists who took time to review sections of the text. Needless to say, I remain responsible for any errors.

Special thanks to Mark Adams, Dan Lin, Andrew Lorey, Fiona Pardington, Tristan Russell, Ratno Sardi, and Kim Wirth for permission to use their photographs, and to the Jowitt family to use the late Glenn Jowitt's images.

My most profound thanks as always are to Annie Coombes, for her love and support. This book is for our son, Nicky, who has done a lot of voyaging, but has much more to do.

June 2020

FURTHER READING

[Banks, Joseph]. *The* Endeavour *Journal of Joseph Banks, 1768–1771.* Edited by J. C. Beaglehole. 2 vols. Sydney: State Library of New South Wales/Angus and Robertson, 1963.

Bellwood, Peter. *Man's Conquest of the Pacific.* Auckland: William Collins, 1978.

Bellwood, Peter, James J. Fox, and Darrel Tryon, eds. *The Austronesians: Historical and Comparative Perspectives.* Canberra: Australian National University, 1995.

Brunt, Peter, and Nicholas Thomas, eds. *Oceania.* London: Royal Academy of Arts, 2018.

Buck, Peter H. [Te Rangihiroa]. *Vikings of the Sunrise.* New York: Stokes, 1938.

Cochrane, Ethan E., and Terry L. Hunt, eds. *The Oxford Handbook of Prehistoric Oceania.* Oxford: Oxford University Press, 2018.

[Cook, James]. *The Journals of Captain James Cook.* Edited by J. C. Beaglehole. 3 vols. Cambridge: Cambridge University Press/Hakluyt Society, 1955–1967.

Dampier, William. *A New Voyage Round the World.* 1697. Edited by Nicholas Thomas. London: Penguin, 2020.

Douglas, Bronwen. *Science, Voyages and Encounters in Oceania, 1511–1850.* London: Palgrave, 2014.

Eckstein, Lars, and Anja Schwarz. "The Making of Tupaia's Map." *Journal of Pacific History* 54 (2019): 1–95. See also commentaries in the same volume of the *Journal of Pacific History*, pp. 529–561.

Finney, Ben, ed. *Pacific Navigation and Voyaging.* Wellington: Polynesian Society, 1976.

Finney, Ben, Marlene Among, Chad Babayan, Tai Crouch, Paul Frost, Bernard Kilonsky, Richard Rhodes, et al. *Voyage of Rediscovery: A Cultural Odyssey Through Polynesia.* Berkeley: University of California Press, 1994.

Forster, George. *A Voyage Round the World.* 1777. Edited by Nicholas Thomas and Oliver Berghof. 2 vols. Honolulu: University of Hawai'i Press, 2000.

Forster, Johann Reinhold. *Observations Made During a Voyage Round the World.* 1778. Edited by Nicholas Thomas, Harriet Guest, and Michael Dettelbach. Honolulu: University of Hawai'i Press, 1996.

Golson, Jack, ed. *Polynesian Navigation.* 2 vols. Wellington: Polynesian Society, 1962.

Haddon, Alfred C., and James Hornell. *Canoes of Oceania.* 3 vols. Honolulu: Bishop Museum, 1936–1938. One vol. reprint, 1975.

Hau'ofa, Epeli. *We Are the Ocean: Selected Works.* Honolulu: University of Hawai'i Press, 2008.

Howe, K. R., ed. *Vaka Moana: Voyages of the Ancestors.* Honolulu: University of Hawai'i Press, 2007.

Irwin, Geoffrey. *The Prehistoric Exploration and Colonisation of the Pacific.* Cambridge: Cambridge University Press, 1992.

Kāne, Herb Kawainui. *Voyage: The Discovery of Hawai'i.* Honolulu: Island Heritage, 1976.

Kirch, Patrick Vinton. *On the Road of the Winds: An Archaeological History of the Pacific Islands Before European Contact.* 2nd ed. Berkeley: University of California Press, 2017. n.b. This includes the most extensive bibliography of relevant archaeological and related literature.

Kirch, Patrick Vinton, and Roger C. Green. *Hawaiki, Ancestral Polynesia: An Essay in Historical Anthropology.* Cambridge: Cambridge University Press, 2001.

Levinson, Michael, R. Gerald Ward, and John W. Webb. *The Settlement of Polynesia: A Computer Simulation.* Minneapolis: University of Minnesota Press, 1973.

Lewis, David. *We, the Navigators: The Ancient Art of Landfinding in the Pacific*. Honolulu: University of Hawai'i Press, 1972.

[Morrison, James]. *Mutiny and Aftermath: James Morrison's Account of the Mutiny on the* Bounty *and the Island of Tahiti*. Edited by Vanessa Smith and Nicholas Thomas. Honolulu: University of Hawai'i Press, 2013.

Sand, Christophe, and Stuart Bedford, eds. *Lapita: Ancêtres océaniens, Oceanic Ancestors*. Paris: Somogy/Musée du quai Branly, 2010.

Spate, O. H. K. *The Pacific Since Magellan*. 3 vols. Canberra: Australian National University Press, 1979–1988.

Spriggs, Matthew. *The Island Melanesians*. Oxford: Blackwell, 1997.

Spriggs, Matthew, Douglas E. Yen, Wal Ambrose, Rhys Jones, Alan Thome, and Ann Andrews, eds. *A Community of Culture: The People and Prehistory of the Pacific*. Canberra: Australian National University, 1993.

Thomas, Nicholas. *Discoveries: The Voyages of Captain Cook*. 2nd ed. London: Penguin, 2018.

Thomas, Nicholas, Julie Adams, Billie Lythberg, Maia Nuku, and Amiria Salmond, eds. *Artefacts of Encounter: Cook's Voyages, Colonial Collecting and Museum Histories*. Honolulu: University of Hawai'i Press, 2016.

ILLUSTRATION CREDITS

Illustration Credits

42 'Océanie', *Atlas universel de géographie physique* (Paris, 1854), handcolored engraving.

44 Courtesy of Fiona Pardington and Starkwhite Galleries, Auckland.

60 Mer (Murray Island). Photograph © Kim Wirth.

61 Alamy Images.

66 Photograph © Tristan Russell.

69 Photograph © Tristan Russell.

73 Engravings from Georg Eberhard Rumpf 's *Herbarium Amboinense* (Amsterdam, 1741–55).

77 Courtesy of Ratno Sardi.

83 Photograph © Mark Adams.

85 Photograph © Mark Adams

86 Photograph © Mark Adams.

98 Photograph © Andrew Lorey.

99 Photograph © Andrew Lorey.

107 Photograph © 1982, Glenn Jowitt; reproduced with permission of the Glenn Jowitt Trust, www.jowittphotography.co.nz.

111 Museum of Archaeology and Anthropology, Cambridge.

112 Auckland War Memorial Museum, Tamaki Paenga Hira.

113 Museum of Archaeology and Anthropology, Cambridge.

116 Museum für Völkerkunde, Dresden 75367. Photograph Esther Hoyer.

117 Photograph © 1982, Glenn Jowitt; reproduced with permission of the Glenn Jowitt Trust, www.jowittphotography.co.nz.

119 Engraving from Schouten's *Diarium vel descriptio laboriosissimi,* & molestissimi itineris (Amsterdam, 1648).

121 Museum of Archaeology and Anthropology, Cambridge.

122 Photograph © Andrew Lorey.

123 Photograph John Layard. Museum of Archaeology and Anthropology, Cambridge.

127 Ethnologisches Museum, Berlin. Photograph Mark Adams.

Illustration Credits

128 Photograph F. H. Dufty. Museum of Archaeology and Anthropology, Cambridge.

129 Museum of Archaeology and Anthropology, Cambridge.

144 Museum of Archaeology and Anthropology, Cambridge.

145 Linden Museum, Stuttgart.

146 Linden Museum, Stuttgart.

150 © British Library Board / Bridgeman Images.

151 © British Library Board / Bridgeman Images.

163 Photograph © 1998, Glenn Jowitt; reproduced with permission of the Glenn Jowitt Trust, www.jowittphotography.co.nz.

171 Photograph © Dan Lin.

173 Photograph © Mark Adams.

NOTES

INTRODUCTION

1. Jerick Sablan, "Traditional Seafarers Arrive in Guam," *Pacific Daily News*, May 16, 2016, guampdn.com/story/news/2016/05/16/traditional -seafarers-arrive-guam/84432448/.

2. Epeli Hauʻofa, "Our Sea of Islands," *Contemporary Pacific* 6 (1994): 153. The essay was first published in Vijay Naidu, Eric Waddell, and Epeli Hauʻofa, eds., *A New Oceania* (Suva, Fiji Islands: University of the South Pacific, 1993).

3. [James Morrison], *Mutiny and Aftermath: James Morrison's Account of the Mutiny on the* Bounty *and the Island of Tahiti*, ed. Vanessa Smith and Nicholas Thomas (Honolulu: University of Hawaiʻi Press, 2013), 225.

4. Here, as on other topics, Patrick Kirch's overview is very helpful: *On the Road of the Winds: An Archaeological History of the Pacific Before European Contact*, 2nd ed. (Berkeley: University of California Press, 2017), 48.

5. Kathy Jetñil-Kijiner, "Tell Them," *Iep Jāltok: Poems from a Marshallese Daughter* (Tucson: University of Arizona Press, 2017), 66.

CHAPTER 1: "THE SAME NATION"

1. See O. H. K. Spate, *The Pacific Since Magellan*, vol. 1, *The Spanish Lake* (Canberra: Australian National University Press, 1979), which

remains an authoritative and readable survey of this phase of Pacific history.

2. As well as parts of New Guinea. For an important reassessment of earlier Spanish and other encounters in Oceania, see Bronwen Douglas, *Science, Voyages, and Encounters in Oceania, 1511–1850* (London: Palgrave, 2014).

3. William Dampier, *A New Voyage Round the World*, 1697, ed. Nicholas Thomas (London: Penguin, 2020), 251.

4. For general background, and on the voyages of Cook specifically, see Nicholas Thomas, *Discoveries: The Voyages of Captain Cook*, 2nd ed. (London: Penguin, 2018).

5. Anne Salmond's studies have been particularly important and influential. See, for example, *The Trial of the Cannibal Dog: Captain Cook in the South Seas* (London: Penguin, 2003).

6. [James Cook], *The Journals of Captain James Cook*, ed. J. C. Beaglehole, vol. 1, *The Voyage of the* Endeavour, *1768–1771* (Cambridge: Cambridge University Press/Hakluyt Society, 1955), 169.

7. Cook, *Journals*, 1:286.

8. Cook, *Journals*, 1:288.

9. [Joseph Banks], *The* Endeavour *Journal of Joseph Banks, 1768–1771*, ed. J. C. Beaglehole (Sydney: Angus and Robertson, 1963), 2:239–41.

10. [James Cook], *The Journals of Captain James Cook*, ed. J. C. Beaglehole, vol. 2, *The Voyage of the* Resolution *and the* Adventure, *1772–1775* (Cambridge: Cambridge University Press/Hakluyt Society, 1955), 354.

11. Cook, *Journals*, 2:264.

12. Johann Reinhold Forster, *Observations Made During a Voyage Round the World*, 1778, eds. Nicholas Thomas, Harriet Guest, and Michael Dettelbach (Honolulu: University of Hawai'i Press, 1996).

13. Forster, *Observations*, 153.

14. See, among other studies, Douglas, *Science, Voyages, and Encounters*.

15. Dumont d'Urville's essay was "Sur les îles du Grand Océan," *Bulletin de la Société de Géographie* 17 (1832): 1–21. Discussions include Nicholas Thomas, *In Oceania: Visions, Artefacts, Histories* (Durham, NC: Duke University Press, 1997); *Journal of Pacific History* 38, no. 2

(2003), a special issue dedicated to "Dumont d'Urville's divisions of Oceania"; and Douglas, *Science, Voyages, and Encounters*.

16. Abraham Fornander, *An Account of the Polynesian Race, Its Origins and Migrations, and the Ancient History of the Hawaiian People to the Times of Kamehameha I* (London: Trübner, 1878). For commentary on Fornander, see, for example, Christina Thompson, *Sea People: In Search of the Ancient Navigators of the Pacific* (London: Collins, 2019), 150–160.

17. Fornander, *An Account*, 48.

18. Fornander, *An Account*, 38.

19. George Eliot, *Middlemarch*, chapter 48.

20. Fornander, *An Account*, x.

21. It is a long-standing point of concern among people in Hawai'i, and those connected with the institution in particular, that it is known as Bishop Museum, not "the Bishop Museum"—the point being to avoid any misidentification with a male church leader. The museum is a foundation in honor of Princess Bernice Pauahi Bishop (1831–1884) of the Hawaiian royal family, and it incorporates what was her private collection.

22. The monographs listed were all published by Bishop Museum. This draws on Patrick Vinton Kirch, *On the Road of the Winds: An Archaeological History of the Pacific Islands Before European Contact*, 2nd. ed. (Berkeley: University of California Press, 2017), 20–23.

23. Peter H. Buck [Te Rangihiroa], *Vikings of the Sunrise* (New York: Stokes, 1938; Christchurch: Whitcombe and Tombs, 1964). Citations refer to the Whitcombe and Tombs edition, which is online at http://nzetc.victoria.ac.nz/tm/scholarly/tei-BucViki.html.

24. Hiroa, *Vikings of the Sunrise*, 15

25. Hiroa, *Vikings of the Sunrise*, 17.

26. Hiroa, *Vikings of the Sunrise*, 17.

27. Quoted in Kirch, *On the Road of the Winds*, 21.

28. Hiroa, *Vikings of the Sunrise*, 19.

29. Hiroa, *Vikings of the Sunrise*, vii.

30. Senghor, first president of independent Senegal, was also a poet and cultural theorist of "Négritude," a black consciousness movement of the decolonization period.

CHAPTER 2: FIRST CROSSINGS

1. This chapter is informed particularly by two outstanding archaeological syntheses: Kirch, *On the Road of the Winds*, chapters 2 and 3; and Matthew Spriggs, *The Island Melanesians* (Oxford: Blackwell, 1997).

2. Alfred Russel Wallace (1823–1913) was one of the most important and influential naturalists of the nineteenth century. The "line" was identified during his travels in island Southeast Asia from 1854 to 1862, published in Alfred Russel Wallace, *The Malay Archipelago* (London: Macmillan, 1869).

3. See Anne Musser, "*Diprotodon optatum*," Australian Museum, last updated March 14, 2019, https://australianmuseum.net.au/learn /australia-over-time/extinct-animals/diprotodon-optatum/.

4. Dylan Gaffney, "Pleistocene Water Crossings and Adaptive Flexibility Within the *Homo* Genus," *Journal of Archaeological Research* (2020).

5. Thomas Sutikna et al., "Revised Stratigraphy and Chronology for *Homo floresiensis* at Liang Bua, Indonesia," *Nature* 532 (2016): 336–369. This publication importantly refines the age range: whereas it was previously thought that the hobbits lived in the area from about ninety-five thousand years ago until as recently as twelve thousand years ago, implying an extended period of coexistence with anatomically modern humans, reinterpretation of the deposits indicates a range of around one hundred thousand to sixty thousand years before the present. For earlier accounts, see Sue O'Connor and Peter Hiscock, "The Peopling of Sahul and Near Oceania," in *The Oxford Handbook of Prehistoric Oceania*, eds. Ethan E. Cochrane and Terry L. Hunt (Oxford: Oxford University Press, 2018), 30–31; and K. L. Baab, "*Homo floresiensis*: Making Sense of the Small-Bodied Hominin Fossils from Flores," *Nature Education Knowledge* 3, no. 9 (2012): 4.

6. F. Détroit et al., "A New Species of *Homo* from the Late Pleistocene of the Philippines," *Nature* 568 (2019): 181–186.

7. Robin W. Dennell et al., "The Origins and Persistence of *Homo floresiensis* on Flores: Biogeographical and Ecological Perspectives," *Quaternary Science Reviews* 96 (2014): 98–107.

8. Michael I. Bird et al., "Early Human Settlement of Sahul Was Not an Accident," *Scientific Reports* 9 (2019): 8220.

9. O'Connor and Hiscock, "The Peopling of Sahul," 34–35.

10. So named because this region, together with the northern part of what is now Papua New Guinea, was under German control from the late nineteenth century to the First World War.

11. Spriggs, *Island Melanesians*, 25–26.

12. Kirch, *On the Road of the Winds*, 55–56.

13. O'Connor and Hiscock, "The Peopling of Sahul," 29–30.

14. Spriggs, *Island Melanesians*, 27–30.

15. Though if dugout canoes were regularly fashioned, adze-like tools ought to be present in the archaeological record, which they are not, from the region and period.

16. Bird et al., "Early Human Settlement."

17. Maxime Aubert et al., "Earliest Hunting Scene in Prehistoric Art," *Nature* 576 (2019): 442–445.

18. Sue O'Connor, Rintaro Ono, and Chris Clarkson, "Pelagic Fishing at 42,000 Years Before the Present and the Maritime Skills of Modern Humans," *Science* 334 (2011): 1117–1121.

19. Spriggs, *Island Melanesians*, 29–30.

20. Spriggs, *Island Melanesians*, 27–28.

21. O'Connor and Hiscock, "The Peopling of Sahul," 41.

22. Kirch, *On the Road of the Winds*, 68–69.

CHAPTER 3: MAKING CONNECTIONS

1. This is the Shung Ye Museum of Formosan Aborigines: see "About Museum," Shung Ye Museum of Formosan Aborigines, www.museum .org.tw/symm_en/01.htm.

2. Christophe Sand, "Oceanic Origins: The History of Research on the Lapita Tradition," in *Lapita: Ancêtres océaniens, Oceanic Ancestors*, eds. Christophe Sand and Stuart Bedford (Paris: Somogy/Musée du quai Branly, 2010), 33. See also Kirch, *On the Road of the Winds*, 23–25. This chapter is especially indebted to the Sand and Bedford volume, and to Kirch, *On the Road of the Winds*, especially chapter 4.

3. Sand, "Oceanic Origins," 33–35; Jack Golson, "Report on New Zealand, Western Polynesia, New Caledonia and Fiji," *Asian Perspectives* 5 (1961):166–180.

4. The literature is extensive; see the bibliography in Sand and Bedford, *Lapita*. Spriggs's survey essay of the 1980s remains important, notwithstanding the range of subsequent research: Matthew Spriggs, "The Lapita Cultural Complex: Origins, Distribution, Contemporaries and Successors," *Journal of Pacific History* 19 (1984): 202–223. At the time of writing, the most up-to-date synthesis is Kirch, *On the Road of the Winds*, chapter 4.

5. Several publications by R. A. Blust have been seminal: see Blust, "The Prehistory of Austronesian-Speaking Peoples: A View from Language," *Journal of World Prehistory* 9 (1995): 453–510; and discussion in Kirch, *On the Road of the Winds*, 79–80.

6. For comparative studies, see Peter Bellwood, James J. Fox, and Darrel Tryon, eds., *The Austronesians: Historical and Comparative Perspectives* (Canberra: Australian National University, 1995); Margaret Jolly and Mark S. Mosko, eds., *Transformations of Hierarchy: Structure, History and Horizon in the Austronesian World* (Basel, Switzerland: Harwood Academic, 1994).

7. Kirch, *On the Road of the Winds*, 80.

8. On affinities, see Roger C. Green, "Early Lapita Art from Polynesia and Island Melanesia: Continuities in Ceramic, Barkcloth and Tattoo Decorations," in *Exploring the Visual Art of Oceania*, ed. Sidney M. Mead (Honolulu: University of Hawai'i Press, 1979), 13–31. For Pacific barkcloth and fiber arts more generally, see Nicholas Thomas, *Oceanic Art*, 2nd ed. (London: Thames and Hudson, 2018), chapter 6.

9. For tattoo (in the context of cross-cultural encounter), see Nicholas Thomas, Anna Cole, and Bronwen Douglas, eds., *Tattoo: Bodies, Art and Exchange in the Pacific and the West* (Durham, NC: Duke University Press, 2005). The most substantial corpus of Lapita designs is published in Sand and Bedford, *Lapita*.

10. Kirch, *On the Road of the Winds*, 81.

11. For the most sustained effort to reconstruct "ancestral Polynesia," see Patrick Vinton Kirch and Roger C. Green, *Hawaiki, Ancestral Polynesia: An Essay in Historical Anthropology* (Cambridge: Cambridge University Press, 2001).

12. Kirch, *On the Road of the Winds*, 209–210.

13. Forster, *Observations*, 231.

14. Anthropologists have long responded to the opportunities for comparative social analysis that the diversification of Polynesian societies appears to afford. See, for example, Irving Goldman, *Ancient Polynesian Society* (Chicago: University of Chicago Press, 1970). My own study of early Marquesan political forms, *Marquesan Societies: Inequality and Political Transformation in Eastern Polynesia* (Oxford: Clarendon Press, 1990), was part of an effort to move away from such "evolutionary" understanding, toward seeing Pacific societies more historically, as local formations responsive to a range of social and environmental dynamics.

15. Among important surveys: Steven Hooper, *Pacific Encounters: Art and Divinity in Polynesia* (Honolulu: University of Hawaiʻi Press, 2006); Peter Brunt et al., *Art in Oceania: A New History* (London: Thames and Hudson, 2012).

16. Banks, Endeavour *Journal*, 2:24.

17. Brunt et al., *Art in Oceania*, 72–73; Peter Brunt and Nicholas Thomas, eds., *Oceania* (London: Royal Academy of Arts, 2018), 281.

18. For the exhibition catalogue, see Brunt and Thomas, *Oceania*. The exhibition was in London from Septemer to December 2018 and at the Musée du quai Branly-Jacques Chirac in Paris from March to July 2019. The event referred to took place in the context of Islander blessings on September 24, 2018, ahead of the opening to the public.

CHAPTER 4:
"THE BEST OF ANY BOATS IN THE WORLD"

1. Dampier, *A New Voyage*, 254.

2. Dampier, *A New Voyage*, 254–255.

3. Alexander Dalrymple, *An Historical Collection of the Several Voyages and Discoveries in the South Pacific Ocean* (London: printed by the author, 1770), 2:17–18.

4. Dalrymple, *An Historical Collection*, 18.

5. Dalrymple, *An Historical Collection*, 22.

6. Fergus Clunie, "*Tongiaki* to *Kalia*: The Micronesian-Rigged Voyaging Canoes of Fiji and Western Polynesia, and Their Tangaloan-Rigged

Forebears," *Journal of the Polynesian Society* 124 (2015): 335–418. The author himself acknowledges that this article traverses a bewildering range of historical, geographical, and cultural factors. Although speculative, it points toward scope for much further research on the deeper history of Oceanic maritime technologies and their complex histories.

7. George Forster, *A Voyage Round the World*, 1777, eds. Nicholas Thomas and Oliver Berghof (Honolulu: University of Hawai'i Press, 2000), 1:251.

8. [James Cook], *The Journals of Captain James Cook*, ed. J. C. Beaglehole, vol. 3, *Voyage of the* Resolution *and* Discovery, *1776–1780* (Cambridge: Cambridge University Press/Hakluyt Society, 1967), part 1, 220.

9. Richard Parkinson, *Thirty Years in the South Seas*, 1907, ed. B. Ankermann, trans. John Dennison (Honolulu: University of Hawai'i Press, 1999), 194–195. The canoe referred to has been moved to Berlin's new museum of world cultures at the Humboldt Forum.

10. Andrew Sharp, *Ancient Voyagers in the Pacific* (Wellington: Polynesian Society, 1956; London: Penguin, 1957). Some later editions titled *Ancient Voyagers in Polynesia*.

11. Jack Golson, "Charles Andrew Sharp (1906–1974)," *Journal of Pacific History* 9 (1974): 131–133.

12. Kirch, *On the Road of the Winds*, 204–208.

13. Jack Golson, ed., *Polynesian Navigation* (Wellington: Polynesian Society, 1962) brought together extended and considered responses.

14. The continuing work of the Polynesian Voyaging Society has been extensively discussed. Though not representing more recent voyages, the best overview is that of Ben Finney et al., *Voyage of Rediscovery: A Cultural Odyssey Through Polynesia* (Berkeley: University of California Press, 1994). See also Ben Finney, *Sailing in the Wake of the Ancestors: Reviving Polynesian Voyaging* (Honolulu: Bishop Museum Press, 2003); and the society's website, www.hokulea.com.

15. Atholl Anderson, "Seafaring in Remote Oceania: Traditionalism and Beyond in Maritime Technology and Migration," in *The Oxford Handbook of Prehistoric Oceania*, eds. Ethan E. Cochrane and Terry L. Hunt (Oxford: Oxford University Press, 2018).

16. Anderson, "Seafaring in Remote Oceania," 486.

CHAPTER 5: KNOWING THE OCEAN

1. John Williams, *A Narrative of Missionary Enterprises in the South Sea Islands* (London: John Snow, 1838), 97–98.

2. Finney et al., *Voyage of Rediscovery*; David Lewis, *We, the Navigators: The Ancient Art of Landfinding in the Pacific* (Honolulu: University of Hawai'i Press, 1972).

3. The following exposition draws on Finney, *Voyage of Rediscovery*, 52–65.

4. Brett Hilder, "Primitive Navigation in the Pacific," in *Polynesian Navigation*, ed. Jack Golson (Auckland: Polynesian Society, 1962), 84–88.

5. Finney, *Voyage of Rediscovery*, 60–61.

6. Forster, *Observations*, 310–311.

7. Key earlier discussions include G. M. Dening, "The Geographical Knowledge of the Polynesians and the Nature of Inter-Island Contact," in *Polynesian Navigation*, ed. Jack Golson (Auckland: Polynesian Society, 1962), 102–131.

8. And notoriously owned in the twentieth century by Marlon Brando.

9. "Geographical Knowledge of the Tahitians," in *Polynesian Navigation*, ed. Jack Golson (Auckland: Polynesian Society, 1962), 132–136.

10. Cook, *Journals*, 1:156–157.

11. Lars Eckstein and Anja Schwarz, "The Making of Tupaia's Map: A Story of the Extent and Mastery of Polynesian Navigation, Competing Systems of Wayfinding on James Cook's *Endeavour*, and the Invention of an Ingenious Cartographic System," *Journal of Pacific History* 54 (2019): 1–95. This extended essay usefully includes extensive citations to the earlier literature on the chart; it should be read in conjunction with commentary by other scholars including Atholl Anderson and Anne Salmond, and a response by Eckstein and Schwarz in *Journal of Pacific History* 54 (2019): 529–561.

12. Eckstein and Schwarz, "The Making of Tupaia's Map," 45.

13. Edward Robarts, *The Marquesan Journal of Edward Robarts*, ed. Greg Dening (Canberra: Australian National University Press, 1974), 266.

14. Morrison, *Mutiny and Aftermath*, 224.

15. Cook, *Journals*, 3:86–87.

16. Hau'ofa, "Our Sea of Islands," 153–155.

INDEX

Index

© ANNIE COOMBES

NICHOLAS THOMAS is professor of historical anthropology at the University of Cambridge and director of the Cambridge Museum of Archaeology and Anthropology. Originally from Australia, he has written and edited numerous books, including *Islanders: The Pacific in the Age of Empire*, for which he was awarded the Wolfson History Prize in 2011. He lives in London.